Women, Power, and the Biology of Peace

Judith L. Hand, Ph.D.

Questpath Publishing
San Diego, California

Questpath Publishing, P.O. Box 270074, San Diego, CA 92198-2074

Copyright © 2003, 2008 by Judith Hand

More information about this title is available at www.questpath.com

All rights reserved. This book, or parts thereof, may not be reproduced or transmitted in any form or by any means without written permission of the publisher, except where permitted by law. Contact Questpath Publishing by mail or fax: 858/485-8001.

Text and cover design and layout by Robert Goodman, Silvercat®, San Diego, California

Cover illustration by Peggy Lang

From *The Argument Culture* by Deborah Tannen, copyright © 1997 by Deborah Tannen. Used by permission of Random House, Inc.

From *Anatomy Of Love: The Natural History of Monogamy, Adultery, and Divorce* by Helen E. Fisher. Copyright © 1992 by Helen E. Fisher. Used by permission of W. W. Norton & Company, Inc.

From web page of Peggy Reeves Sanday. Used by permission of Peggy Reeves Sanday.

Reprinted with the permission of The Free Press, a Division of Simon & Schuster, Adult Publishing Group, from *The End Of History And The Last Man* by Francis Fukuyama. Copyright © 1992 by Francis Fukuyama.

Excerpts from *On Aggression* by Konrad Lorenz, copyright ©1963 by Dr. G. Bortha-Schoeler Verlag, Wein, English translation by Majorie Kerr Wilson, copyright © 1966 by Konrad Lorenz, reprinted by permission of Harcourt, Inc.

Copyright for Barn Swallows, Girl with Curly Hair, and Girl with Shaved Hair from *Art and Religion in Thera* by Nanno Marinatos held by D. & I. Mathioulakis, Athens, Greece.

Copyright for The Procession, The Prince, and Blue Bird from *In The Days Of King Minos* by Lyda Krontira held by Ekdotike Athenon S. A., Athens, Greece.

Copyright for Snake Goddesses from *Dawn of the Gods* by Jaquetta Hawkes held by A.D. Peters, Adelphi, London, England.

Hand, Judith, 1940-
Women, power, and the biology of peace / Judith Hand p. cm.
Includes bibliographical references, illustrations, and index. ISBN 0-9700031-6-1 (softcover)
ISBN 0-9700031-5-3 (hardcover)
1. Women and war. 2. War and society. 3. War (Philosophy) 4. Peace (Philosophy) 5. Sex differences (Psychology) I. Title
HQ1233.H32 2003   305.42
                                                QBI03-200343

Second Edition, 2008
Printed in the United States of America

*This book is dedicated to
Jane Goodall and E. O. Wilson,
two of my heroes,*

*And with grateful love
to my greatest hero,
my husband and best friend,
Harold Hand.*

Judith Hand earned her Ph.D. in biology from UCLA where her studies included training in animal behavior and primatology. She subsequently spent a year as a Smithsonian Post-doctoral Fellow at the National Zoo in Washington, D.C., and then returned to UCLA as a research associate and lecturer. Her undergraduate major was in cultural anthropology. As a student of animal communication, she has written on the subject of social conflict resolution. She has also worked as a technician in neurophysiology laboratories at UCLA and the Max Planck Institute, in Munich, Germany.

She has written several novels and a screenplay, all of which feature strong female heroines. To research the historical novel *Voice of the Goddess,* Dr. Hand worked at the archeological museum on Crete and visited temple sites at Knossos, Phaestos, and Gournia. She interviewed the principal investigator of the Minoan excavation on Santorini (Thera) and visited museum and goddess sites in Turkey.

An avid camper, classical music fan, and birdwatcher, she currently lives in Rancho Bernardo, California.

For more information about the book, the author, or how to contact her, see her web site, <www.jhand.com>.

Contents

Foreword ix
Acknowledgments xi
Preface xiii
Introduction 17

Section I - Biology

A Female Priority For Stability Vs. A Male Priority
To Invade And Conquer 25

    Martian Men And Venusian Women 25
    The Biological Logic 26
    The Genetics of Inclinations 29
    Inclinations and the Bell Curve 31

Modern Research and Gender Differences 35

    Differences in Brain Structure 35
    Differences in Brain Function 38
    Studies on Infants and Cross-cultural Studies of Children . 39
    The Outer Boundaries of Human Nature 43
    Summary of the Central Hypothesis of *Women, Power,*
    and the Biology of Peace 44

Section II – A Powerful, Creative Civilization without War – Is That Possible?

The Keftian Way 49

    Comparing State-level Civilizations 50
    The Keftians – Who, When, Where 51
    Matriarchy And Use of Power 51
        Matriarchy? 51
        Use of Power – Making Decisions for the Community 53
        How Women Use Power 55
    Who's Your Mother and Where Do You Live? 56
        Matrilineality 56
        Matrilocality 58
    Art and Artifacts 59
        Women at Least Equal to Men in Influence 60
        A Sophisticated Culture 64
        Peace 66
    Why Only The Keftians 70
        Six Necessary Conditions 70

Section III – Regulating Social Behavior

Regulating Social Behavior 77

    Shunning 77
    A Sacred Sex Hypothesis 79
        Evidence from Biology – Chimpanzees and Bonobos 79
        Evidence from Anthropology – The Canela of
            South America 84
        Evidence from the Keftians – The Keftian
            Snake Goddesses 85
        Evidence from the Tradition of Sacred Prostitution 87
    The Ideal Of Romantic Love 88

Section IV – Women And Warfare

Women and Warfare 93

Agricultural Revolution and the Shift in the Balance
of Power between the Sexes 93
Women As Warriors 95
Defense vs. Offense 97
Women, Cycles of Defense (Revenge), and
Raiding for Resources 105
Breaking Free 108

Section V – Waging Peace

A Vision of a Peaceful Future and How to Get There 113

Taming the Male Urge to Dominate 114
Hidden Females - To Solve a Problem We
Need to Know What the Problem Is 114
Francis Fukuyama's *The End of History*
and the Last Man 121
Two Engines of History 121
The Scientific Method 121
The Need for Recognition 123
A Critique of Fukuyama's Hypothesis 124
Hidden Females 124
The need for Connectedness (Positively Met)
and the End of History 125
Looking for Guidance 129
What to Do With Young Men? 131
Moving From "Win-Lose" Cultures to
Cultures of "Mutual Gain" 134
Anticipating Problems 136

Empowering Women 136
   Empowerment Beyond the Political. 138
      Educationally 138
      Economically 139
      The Laws 140
      Religion... 140
      Worldwide... 141
   Predicting The Future 141
   A World of Empowered Women 143
   Blame and Choice 146
   Back To Balance.. 148
      The Study of Existing Women-centered Cultures 148
      Positive Aspects of Aggression 151
      Balance 152

Appendix 1 – Organizations Dedicated to Empowering
   Women Worldwide 155
Appendix 2 – Ways to Participate in Waging Peace 159
Selected References and Additional
   Recommended Reading 163
Bibliography 169
Index... 175

Figures and Tables

Figure 1: The Bull Leapers.. 60
Figure 2: The Procession.. 61
Figure 3: The Prince 63
Figure 4: Temple at Knossos 65
Figure 5: The Swallows.. 66
Figure 6: The Bluebird... 66
Figure 7: Girl from Akrotiri 67
Figure 8: Girl with Shaved Head.................................. 67

Figure 9: The Harvester Vase 67
Figure 10: Snake Goddesses 87

Table 1: Reasons Women Took Up Arms 101
Table 2: Conquerors vs. Revolutionaries 103

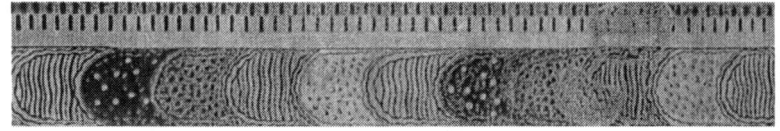

Foreword

War will not be eliminated in the foreseeable future, if ever.
> Robert S. McNamara
Former US Secretary of Defense
LA Times, Aug. 3, 2003

Can humans create a future without war? Many people don't think so.

What if "many people" are wrong? Unless we believe, we cannot achieve. Until thinkers, leaders, and ordinary people root out and disown the unquestioned pessimism expressed by Secretary McNamara, we are doomed to repeat our past.

The goal of a warless future can, in fact, be achieved. Judith Hand demonstrates this succinctly in her compelling exploration of war, peace, and the interplay of biology and human nature.

Dr. Hand acknowledges that "we will never be without conflict." And why should we? "Conflict is actually good for us. Like variety, it's one of the spices of life. Conflict is a critical ingredient of friendships and humor, an essential element in things we find exciting, from reading fiction to finding a mate."

Women, Power, and the Biology of Peace

A future without war is not a future without conflict, which is an inescapable source of creative energy. But Hand explains how we can—indeed, *must*—change the way we deal with conflict so that "war becomes a bad memory from a brutal past." Conflict may be inherently human, but "war is not part of our nature. We *can* eliminate war."

Women, Power, and the Biology of Peace is a hopeful book, a must read for all of us. No one can afford to ignore this eloquent, informed, intelligent celebration of the human spirit.

>Robert L. Goodman, Ph.D., Past President
>Publishers & Writers of San Diego
>author of "**Newbury, Massachusetts, 1635-1685:
>The Social Foundations of Harmony and Conflict**"

A Future Without War.
   Believe in it,
   envision it,
   work for it,
And we will achieve it.

     Judith Hand
     www.AFutureWithoutWar.org

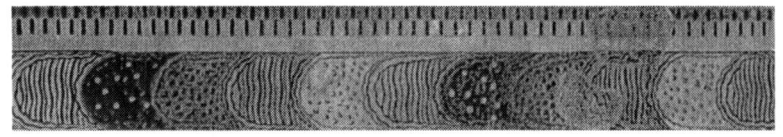

Acknowledgments

Women, Power, and the Biology of Peace owes its existence to my friend and colleague, Peggy Lang. From the moment she heard me cover the subject in short form in a speech, she unswervingly encouraged and supported its creation. Her editing comments were invaluable and her enthusiasm critical to keeping me going.

I was also generously given the time of individuals who read and criticized various sections or full drafts: Stephanie Budin, Drusilla Campbell, Mark Clements, Donna Erickson, Barry Friedman, Robert Goodman, Sara Blaffer Hrdy, Joseph Jehl, Pete Johnson, Deanna LeCoco, Sheila Mahoney, Raymond Pierotti, Jay Sheppard, and Paul Shen-Brown. Not all of them agree with everything I have to say, and I am solely responsible for the ideas, but the comments of all greatly improved my effort.

I extend a special "thank you" to the authors of the secondary sources I relied on which are listed in the bibliography. I chose these references with care and with the intention that, if at all possible, the references I cited should be accessible to the book's readers from any good local library. These authors marshaled their expertise to bring together the knowledge of their field and put it into books that can spread highly specialized information to a vast readership. We are all beholden to writers who have this special talent for making the arcane accessible to us all.

I also take this opportunity to recognize my debt to the thousands of scientists and other specialists listed in the extensive bibliographies of these secondary sources. These are the trenchermen, those lovers of knowledge and the quest for truth who dedicated years of toil, sometimes in extraordinarily difficult circumstances, in the search for knowledge. The Jane Goodalls, E. O. Wilsons, Jared Diamonds, and thousands of names we don't recognize, all of whom have done their part to bring light where there was darkness. To them goes my most profound gratitude.

And finally, I am grateful to Robert Goodman, who spent precious hours critiquing the ideas and editing the writing, pushing me so that the book would be my best effort. And then provided the beautiful layout and design of the interior and cover.

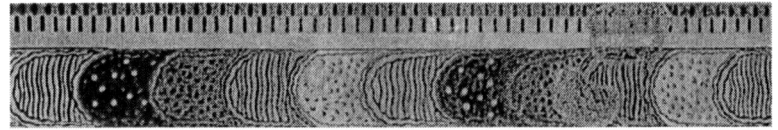

Preface

Women. Power. Peace. This book explores how these three relate to each other.

In a 2002 address at the University of California, Davis, the American ex-president, Bill Clinton, described his vision of what it will take for the world's people to secure a more peaceful future. He described national behavior and policies that stoke hostility and aggression. He described positions and actions required of a nation that seeks to create more partners in the world and fewer enemies.

I select Clinton's speech as an example of today's political thinking in order to point out that, though well-intentioned, the current visions of our most visionary politicians remain inadequate. His insights reflected his intellect, experience, and the thoughts of a well-read, serious thinker. Nevertheless, I noted that he didn't acknowledge that over four thousand years of recorded history conclusively demonstrates that governance by men in complex societies, in any form, has never yet yielded lasting peace. Nor did he give his audience reason to believe our time in history will be different.

He appeared to assume that if we are men and women of good will and work at it, we can finally grasp what has eluded us for millennia. I also noted that at no point did he acknowledge that there are differences, important differences, between men and women with respect to aggression. Nor did he consider how the exclusion of women from decision-making in world affairs may have impacted our fates. It is this specific issue—exclusion of one gender and the resulting effect on war and peace—that is the subject of this book.

Before going forward, I acknowledge that some people argue that a bit of war now and then is a beneficial evil, a necessary engine that drives creativity of all sorts. I make no attempt to argue the pros and cons of that view. I assume that while some wars have, beyond question, been necessary, modern war is an unmitigated tragedy and a waste. It is a demon from our evolutionary past.

There is a danger involving bias I want to address because I'm a female author offering a harsh assessment of male aggression. I've been told by friends and colleagues that the defining features of my life—the disciplines I've studied, the professions I've practiced, the experiences I've had as a woman raised in a male-dominated culture—make me uniquely qualified to write a book on this subject. And important among those qualifications is that for thirty years, until recently widowed, I was happily married to a man I adored. I love men. I do criticize the males of our species, but I also look at females with a critical eye. While the tendencies described are often associated with one gender or the other, I stress that they exist in both sexes. And the book's theme, stated more than once, is that what war-weary humanity needs for best results is male/female partnership.

My purpose is exploration and my point is positive:

(a) a practical and achievable path to peace does exist.
(b) there is a powerful biological underpinning for this path.

Humans are not forever doomed by our nature to be wracked repeatedly by vicious and destructive armed conflicts.

Women, Power, and the Biology of Peace

War—its causes and how culture and biology work together to produce it—is complex. One book, especially a small one, certainly cannot be in any way definitive. My intention in *Women, Power, and the Biology of Peace* is to present a new perspective that I hope will provoke reflection and discussion.

We are living in extraordinary times: as I explore in the pages that follow, the tide of the history of the last ten millennia is turning with respect to the relationships between men and women and war. Each of us will play apart, however small, in the speed with which this revolutionary tide shifts. The land to which it bears us is unknown, but I will argue that, from the perspective of biology, war is not inevitable. It is a choice. We can accept war as our predestination or resolve to be rid of it. A clear understanding of the differing biological predispositions of men and women can be the basis of new cultural imperatives that if achieved, will provide a stabilizing polestar as we journey together to arrive at, to in fact create, a far more peaceful home.

J. L. Hand

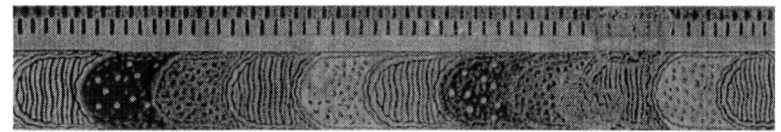

Introduction

> *If women ran the world, there would be no wars.*
>   Winston Churchill

> *If women ran the world, we wouldn't have wars, just intense negotiations every twenty-eight days.*
>   Robin Williams

No wars. Must that dream remain forever a dream? Or can we make it a reality?

Religions haven't tamed this Apocalyptic horseman. Quite the contrary. Pacifism, too, stands powerless against his charge. Secular appeals to humanitarian morality find themselves trampled into the mud and dust of one ravaged land after another. Education also fails, as the Second World War conclusively proved; the Germans were some of the world's most educated people. When War engulfs us, we suffer unimaginable horror and brutality and waste of resources and life in spite of all our moral training and education.

You may have wondered when you sent a son or daughter or soul mate off to fight, or went yourself, if humanity could escape the tragic and brutal cycle of destruction, or if this behavior, as so many have claimed, is in our genes, forever a part of our destiny. You may have thought, "I'd give anything to stop wars," and questioned to the depth of your being if you couldn't personally do something to defeat this dreaded horseman.

In early October, 1992, I had begun a journey that would explore these questions and reveal some answers. I followed the Minoan workshop leader from The First International Minoan Celebration of Partnership out of our meeting room onto the patio of the Akti Zeus Hotel in Heraklion, Crete.

A flawless blue sky arched overhead. Dazzling beds of flowers—yellows, oranges, and reds—welcomed us. We sought refuge from the stark Mediterranean sun under a patio umbrella, taking seats opposite each other.

At once she said, "I asked you to talk with me in private because your comment was upsetting to some of the workshop participants."

Since I had offered only one comment, there could be no doubt about what she was referring to. During a question and answer session, I'd said, "Well, assuming that peaceful goddess societies did once exist and they were supplanted by patriarchal, warlike societies, they likely ceased to exist because they couldn't or wouldn't fight back. Sometimes fighting back is absolutely essential."

This sentiment, apparently, had been so upsetting to some of the Minoan workshop members, a number of whom were pacifists, that our leader felt compelled to ask me to tone down my comments. Which is exactly what she was doing—in a most gentle manner, but firmly.

I agreed to her request. I wasn't there to argue politics or philosophy. But I couldn't help noting that the exchange illustrated how humans are often reluctant to be troubled by facts when their cherished beliefs are challenged.

Riane Eisler, author of *The Chalice and The Blade,* was one of the conference organizers. Many experts continue to disagree with Eisler, who proposes that in ancient times, many "goddess cultures" existed throughout Europe, and that these had been peaceful and egalitarian, and had been conquered, and that most evidence of their existence had been obliterated by patriarchal cultures that succeeded them. Whether one entirely agrees or disagrees, her book is thought-provoking. The second organizer was Margarita Papandreou, former wife of the Greek Prime Minister and a noted pacifist.

The meeting's principal objective was to assemble leaders, women and men, from around the world who shared the views and goals of Eisler and Papandreou. These two women convened this gathering in the hope that participants would cross-pollinate and generate plans of action to advance the world's progress toward a more positive future of partnership between men and women.

My Minoan workshop was a small part of this much larger project. The workshop was, however, headed by world-class experts on a Bronze Age culture that had flourished on Crete some three and a half thousand years ago. Since I was right in the thick of researching a novel set in that long ago time and in this exact place, I couldn't pass up a chance to simultaneously learn from the best and soak up local atmosphere.

Two days after this little talk on the patio, I was strolling alone through the stunning ruins of Knossos outside Heraklion. The excavator of this once lost and still largely unknown culture, the British archaeologist Sir Arthur Evans, had dubbed this site the palace of the mythical Greek king Minos. I arrived at the east side and stood at the base of narrow steps, craned to look upward at several stories of massive cut stone, and then trudged my way to the top. I stepped onto what must have been an entryway and marveled again at the sophistication of the drains carved into the stone. I closed my eyes and in my imagination heard flowing water and saw elegant courtyard gardens richly decorated with sweet-scented flowers.

Four days earlier I had been here on a tour to get a sense of what local guides were telling visitors, but on this day I began my own research at these ruins, and at the fine museum in the town and at other sites on Crete. I wandered through a maze of rooms and courtyards, large and small, and passed through the Great Central Court, where it is thought the important event of Bull Leaping might have been watched by thrilled crowds of hundreds. I studied the partial reconstruction of the impressive Procession mural, knowing that its central figure was a woman. As I explain later, women had been respected here. Most impressively, for hundreds of years they had apparently kept peace here. I walked ancient, sun-warmed stones determined to learn how that might have happened.

I turned a corner and walked toward the middle of what is usually called the West Court. There, coming toward me, was our workshop leader. She, too, was alone. We met in the court's center. Stopped. Smiled. But said nothing. We shared a moment of understanding requiring no words. We were, each of us, in our own ways and with our own visions and needs, communing with the people who had lived and worked and loved and died here all those thousands of years ago.

In the year 2000, I finished my novel, *Voice of the Goddess*. *Women, Power, and the Biology of Peace* began its life as a companion to that work. I wanted to explain for my readers the theoretical background against which I viewed the Minoan civilization, the Bronze Age people who form the flesh and spirit of the novel's world.

I wanted to do this because as I worked on the Minoan fiction, I also explored the possibility that these people were as extraordinary with respect to aggression as Sir Arthur Evans thought they were. If so, the Minoan culture is far more than an interesting, exotic world in which to set an epic novel. If the culture of ancient Crete was as peaceful as the evidence to date indicates, its existence has profound significance for humanity's past, present, and future. These unusual people may have been a state-level civilization in which the fact that women had power made a profound difference when it came to the matter of war. From the depths of the past, the Minoans become a case study of what might have been, and in Part II, I describe and discuss their significance in some detail.

This book's central theme is that lasting world peace cannot be achieved without full partnership between men and women. We need male/female balance in civic affairs. The attendees of the conference on Crete embraced this theme unanimously. But their arguments in support of balance for the most part seemed to me to rest on a sense of morality—that it's not "right" for men to dominate women, particularly because male domination leads to bad results. Moral arguments seldom "work." Rather than look to morality, *Women, Power, and the Biology of Peace* looks to biology to explain why calls to morality have failed to prevent "bad" behavior in the past and will continue to fail in the future.

So, from a biological perspective, how might world history over the last four thousand years or so have been different if women had been running things all these millennia, or if they were to be running things now?

Section I - Biology

How about this for another slogan; 'War is to Man what Motherhood is to Woman?' Very good, I think you'll agree. A fine slogan with a lot of virility to it...

> ❧ The Duce
> ❧ from Louis de Bernieres' *Corelli's Mandolin*

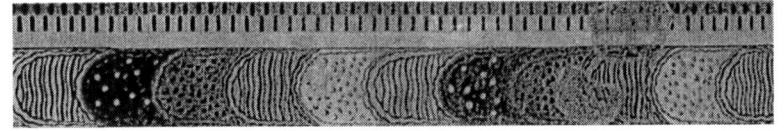

A Female Priority for Stability vs. a Male Priority to Invade and Conquer

Martian Men and Venusian Women

Is there *any* reason to think women would do *anything* differently from what men have done? Many women like to think they would, but liking to think so doesn't make it true—or even likely to be true. If women had power, perhaps its seductive sway would lead them to act exactly like men.

If we look only to American culture, we might infer that women are less aggressive than men and so, surely, they would do things differently. But looking to only one culture and being guided by "gut feelings" easily leads to erroneous thinking. To explore the question of whether significant male/female differences might transcend culture, I start by turning to the field of evolutionary biology.

John Gray has become famous for saying: "Men are from Mars. Women are from Venus." His book by that title, one of the most popular relationship books, suggests how men and women can understand their differences in order to communicate better and get along.

Some differences Gray describes are what anthropologists can demonstrate to be superficial (changing fashion can quickly alter them) or they are cultural (not based on genetics and thus changeable, although often not readily). But this familiar phrase also expresses a significant kernel of biological truth. Some differences between men and women have deep genetic origins and are, for all practical considerations, unchangeable.

Evolutionary biologists have for years been exploring what they call male and female reproductive strategies. I focus here on the work of Sara Blaffer Hrdy, an anthropologist whose specialty is primate social behavior. She has written several impressive survey books, the latest of which is **Mother Nature**. This sterling piece of academic writing, scrupulously documented and so well written it's quite accessible to lay readers, presents in detail a list of references as well as the kind of evidence that forms the backbone of the following steps of biological logic. Another excellent and brief discussion of most of these biological points is Deborah Blum's introduction to her book, *Sex on the Brain.*

The Biological Logic

Keep in mind two biological facts: first, we are mammals and, like all female mammals, our females produce milk to feed their offspring. And second, we're primates, related to chimpanzees, gorillas, and orangutans and more distantly to baboons and monkeys. Keeping these biological facts in mind, the biological logic goes like this:

> 1. For all living things, the **basic biological bottom line is to reproduce and have offspring that in turn have offspring.** Genes of individuals that fail to reproduce are eliminated from the great evolutionary game of life. This means that the behavioral inclinations coded in those genes are not passed to subsequent generations. There are some subtleties here—

for example, highly social animals (bees, humans) can often contribute some genes to the future by aiding close relatives who possess the same genes rather than reproducing themselves—but such subtleties don't alter the basic biological reality.

2. For female mammals, and certainly **for female primates, reproducing successfully is a very expensive proposition.** Female primates carry an offspring to term, protecting and nourishing it within their body, often for many months. Then they provide milk to nourish it for weeks if not months or even years more. They must protect it, care for it, and support it sometimes for many additional years before it is old enough to reproduce. For every parent raising children, whether in the United States, Brazil, Thailand, or Ghana, the extensive costs involved (in time, energy, risk, and resources) resonate deeply. And then, in most cultures, once a child is raised, females remain involved in ensuring that the offspring of their offspring—their grandchildren—also survive. This is, beyond doubt or argument, an extraordinarily expensive process.

3. As a consequence of the above, the **ideal condition for female primates** to carry out this difficult and expensive feat **is social stability for long periods.** Serious social turmoil or anything that threatens the life of these expensive offspring before they can reproduce—and certainly war that results in their death or the death or loss of their primary caregiver, their mother—is hugely counterproductive.

4. For **male mammals,** including male primates, the biological game is usually quite different, because they **do not invest as heavily in the survival of their children as females do.** In some primates, fathers contribute little or nothing beyond their sperm. While human males often become involved in support and protection of their young, this isn't the case in all cultures (see, for example, the Mosuo described by Hua where technically there isn't even an institution

of marriage), and in few cultures does a father's investment approach that of a mother. There are some notable primate exceptions, tamarins for example, but compared to females, male mammals including male primates are generally more involved in spreading their seed widely than investing heavily in any given offspring.

5. Consequently, **for male primates, social stability is not as high a priority** as it is for females. For example, in her first major book, *Infanticide,* written with colleague Glenn Hausfater, Hrdy documents a number of cases where males form a group or team and move into an established troop, drive out or kill the resident males, and then kill the young—that is, these males invade and subsequently commit infanticide. Even males of other mammalian species, like lions, behave similarly.

Killing the young means that their mothers stop suckling and begin their estrous (menstrual) cycles again so that they are fertile. For the invading males this means they can breed sooner than if they had tolerated the offspring of the vanquished males. By cooperating in this group action, an invading male increases his chances of gaining access to the premier biological resource for a male: a female or females he can impregnate.

Group male aggression can also give males access to other resources on a captured territory: food, water, new places to shelter. No one questions that it facilitates protection of the group from predators and enables many types of hunting. The potential benefits of male cooperative aggression are multiple and great.

From *Mother Nature* and *Infanticide* you can form your own assessment of the power of competition for resources such as food, territory, or access to females, to shape the evolution in many primates of a male tendency to band together for invasion. In my view, **while human males may have evolved under an imperative to** invade and conquer, a basic reproductive imperative for females has been to do whatever they can to foster social stability. I propose that a female inclination to facilitate social stability is as deeply evolved in humans as the well-known and frequently discussed male inclination for group aggression.

This is why things would be different if women ran the world—specifically, society would be more socially stable. Because of a female's unavoidable and costly commitment to her offspring, basic human female biological priorities are different from those of males.

These differences are not cultural. Their origins are deeply rooted in our evolutionary past. We inherit them from our pre-human primate ancestors. Given free rein and uncurbed by social or ecological forces, these opposed tendencies—with males ready to bond together in acts of aggression and females more inclined to seek social stability—will play themselves out in our group behavior. Not to take them into consideration when discussing the question of war and how to make a lasting peace is a profound error.

The Genetics of Inclinations

There is no gene for "doing war," no gene for "working toward stability." When it comes to making complex decisions between competing choices, genes aren't at all directly involved. Rather, they affect behavior by directing the construction of brains and endocrine organs and sense organs. It takes many genes working in concert to direct the growth and assembly of these body structures, including delicate brain architecture.

Once a brain is constructed during embryonic development, it becomes the body's decision-maker. Environmental stimuli are detected by sense organs—our ears and eyes and so on. The quality or "amount" of a stimulus is coded as electrochemical signals passed along nerve cells to the brain, our CPU (central processing unit).

There, inside our skulls, the brain decodes and manipulates the signals. The location in the brain where these impulses end up determines how the brain interprets the input. Impulses coming from the eyes are interpreted as visual signals. If the signals arrive at the part of the brain linked by neural paths to the nose, the brain interprets the input as smell. All this information from our sense organs is subsequently processed in a variety of complex ways.

One of the results of this processing is often an emotional response. The brain's structure, the result of numberless generations of natural selection, determines whether we experience the stimuli that have come in as pleasing or noxious, delightful or revolting. On a bitterly cold day we find the heat of a campfire pleasing, and the offer of a bowl of ice cream something we can pass up. We feel as we do, not because of single genes for those reactions, but because many genes acting in concert constructed for us sensory organs to pick up information from our environment and a brain that makes those assessments.

Another result of processing can be a decision, a conscious or unconscious one, about how to respond. We huddle closer to the toasty fire. We decline the chilly ice cream.

It is the architecture and chemistry of a human brain that determines which social conditions a given brain finds satisfying, pleasurable, exciting, stimulating, cool, worth doing, worth working for. Such stimuli or conditions are said to be "reinforcing," and they drive our behavior. We respond to positive reinforcers (food, safe hiding place, a good-looking member of the opposite sex) and to negative reinforcers (pain, scolding, social isolation). Our genes guide the construction of brains, and then our brains respond positively to various stimuli and negatively to others.

If evolution produced a male tendency (inclination) for this and a female tendency (inclination) for that, we would find that the brains of males and females respond differently to the same stimulus context—in this case a choice to go to war or not—with males inclined in one direction, females inclined in another.

Inclinations and the Bell Curve

What is quite evident is that differences between men and women in the traits in question are not either/or. It's not that one gender has it while the other doesn't. Both tendencies—the thrill of bonding together to go "kick ass" and the capacity to take pleasure in social stability—are present in both men and women. After all, men who do live in communities with the children they have fathered would benefit by that community remaining secure and stable. And women, as I discuss at some length later, can be roused to fight in defense of their offspring or the community where they are raising their offspring. The question is whether men and women differ sufficiently *on average* in expressing these traits so that letting one or the other sex express its tendency unchecked leads to disastrous results.

Were we to measure the eye color of men and women, from extremely light blue to darkest blue, and plot the number of individuals having a given eye color on a graph, we would find that the curve (distribution) for men and the curve for women would overlap virtually perfectly. There is no significant difference between men and women in eye color.

But if we were to measure the amount of fat and glandular tissue lying between the nipple and the underlying breast muscle in adults, adjusting the measures to account for different levels of obesity, and plot those distributions, the curves would hardly overlap at all. Only a few men have a breast measurement that overlaps those women who develop small breasts. Most men would be completely excluded from overlap with the female curve.

A good way to think about differences between men and women in any trait—height, weight, upper body strength, ability to do math, facility with language, facility with solving spatial problems—is the bell curve. The graphed distribution of the measurements of many individuals having a given ability or trait, when plotted, takes the shape of a bell, with the measurements of a few individuals on either extreme of the curve and the majority of people falling somewhere in the middle.

When no difference exists between two groups, such as men and women, and you place the curve of one group on top of the other, the curves overlap perfectly. If the frequency of occurrence of traits of individuals from the two groups is not the same—if for example, one group has individuals that have much higher scores than any individuals in the other group—the curves will not match. When you try to place one group's curve on top of the other, there will be an offset.

When we plot occurrence frequencies of different traits for men and women, the curves almost always overlap, sometimes a lot, sometimes very little. And that's the heart of the problem here. Just how much do inherited male and female tendencies for engaging in war or striving for social stability match up? If there is a difference, how great is it? And how can we measure such inclinations?

Trying to evaluate the degree of difference becomes particularly complicated because learning profoundly influences the ways humans express these two opposed tendencies. The relationship between learning and expression of the desire to go to war, or instead to make peace, is so complex, it's simply impossible to make direct measures of innate, biologically inherited differences. What we can do is consider approximations, which I do in several sections to follow (**Differences in Brain Structure, Differences in Brain Function, Studies on Infants and Cross-cultural Studies of Children, Women As Warriors,** and **Hidden Females**).

A warning is appropriate here, a reminder. Individual men and women are unique. Wonderfully unique. Each is a distinct, astoundingly complex combination of what members of various cultures **choose** to call male and female traits. How gender differences relate to culture and how personality traits are molded and modified by learning are subjects covered in such texts as *Cultural*

Anthropology by Carol and Melvin Ember or the similarly titled one by William Haviland. One fundamental and clear fact is that through the influence of learning, culture is a powerful determinant of what behavior for adults of the two sexes is considered normal and acceptable.

But culture is not all-powerful. One of the central goals of the Women's Liberation Movement was the struggle to let each person be whatever he or she wants to be—to free individuals from stereotyped expectations imposed by the cultural norms of a particular society that often don't suit the temperament or talents of a given man or woman. The goal was to give scope to the wealth of human individuality.

In *Women, Power, and the Biology of Peace,* however, I'm not focusing on unique individuals. I'm concerned with how statistically significant male/female differences in opposed inclinations relating to war working through large groups of individuals affect the shaping of our cultural lives.

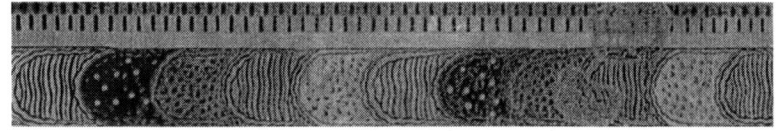

Modern Research and Gender Differences

A veritable mountain of research in the past few decades has put to rest any idea that men and women are born into this world as blank slates upon which culture draws up the person we know as an adult. This *tabula rasa* idea described the notion that nurture was all and nature nothing. Over time, we've learned that humans are not infinitely moldable into whatever shape a society might like to dictate. And the latest research is clear: male and female babies, on average, come out of the womb different and become more so as parents, friends, and culture mold their behavior.

Differences in Brain Structure

One of the most exciting things that can happen to a scientist is to have an epiphany. This can be the extraordinary moment when you learn something entirely new, something no one else in the world yet knows is true—and you are its discoverer. Such a moment is one a scientist lives for. But there is another kind of epiphany: when you are presented with sufficient data to turn your world upside down. That too, is fabulously exciting, even when you may not have been the discoverer. One such experience I've had concerns sex differences and brains.

When I began graduate school, I was absolutely certain that while the bodies of men and women were different, their minds were essentially the same. I could cite you study after study showing how parents treat male and female children differently, causing them to develop differently. I could cite criticisms of studies from the past about brain size that had been used to argue that women were intellectually inferior to men, criticisms that showed clearly how investigator bias—the belief that women were inferior—had influenced the investigator's analysis and conclusions.

I could cite studies showing that even before children are born, we treat boy and girl babies differently and have different expectations for them. I myself vividly recall shopping for a gift for the birth of a nephew. I found a perfect, cuddly outfit. But it was pink, and they didn't have a blue one. I simply could not bring myself to buy pink for a boy. Instead, I settled on a yellow blanket.

And I chalked the experience up to one more example of how our expectations and treatment of the sexes differ, even when we might want to treat them the same. I was utterly convinced that at birth the "minds" of men and women are the same, and that it's just different treatment that explains the differences we see in the behavior and interests of adults.

Then when I was doing Master's work at UCLA, I attended a seminar by Jerre Levy, a young neurobiologist. The subject was brain architecture. Levy claimed to be finding clear differences in the structure of a particular brain area. The clear differences were between the brains of males and females. I remember as if it were yesterday storming enraged out of the seminar. I was furious with Levy, thinking her a traitor to her sex because she was reinforcing the notion that mentally women were different from men—that is, inferior.

But time proved Levy right. I followed the literature through the years until one day my epiphany struck. The weight of the data had become overwhelming and incontrovertible. Here and there, in this slight way and that, male and female brains were different! My world turned upside down. I was going to have to deal with that unsettling fact.

My assumption was wrong, however, that difference would be taken to indicate female inferiority. The brains are simply different. They are not inferior or superior.

The clear implication, however, is that if the brains are built differently, men and women may do some things slightly, or even significantly, differently. We ignore these difference at our peril, because any time we ignore the truth, we are swimming the wrong way in a powerful stream and are in danger of drowning.

Let me describe four sample differences in structure that come from studies of preserved adult brains. Others and references to original research can be found in Helen Fisher's *The First Sex*, Anne Moir and David Jessel's *Brain Sex*, the section on fetal brain development in Linda Mealey's *Sex Differences*, and a particularly thorough discussion in Deborah Blum's *Sex on the Brain*.

- One region of the pre-frontal cortex is larger in women. Fisher believes this may reflect something she calls "web-thinking" in women, versus "step-thinking" in men.
- Women have greater neuron density in the posterior temporal cortex, an area involved in differentiating sounds involved with language processing. This seems to correspond with studies showing that women do, on average, tend to have better linguistic abilities.
- The anterior commissure is 12% bigger in women.
- An area of the corpus collosum is somewhat larger in women.

The last two findings were made fairly early in these new investigations into sex differences in the brain. They are particularly interesting because these two thick bands of tissue, the anterior commissure and corpus collosum, connect the right hemisphere of the brain with the left hemisphere. They are the principle media through which the right and left halves of the brain talk to each other.

The thicker connections in women do seem to relate to a constellation of traits where women seem to be better than men, namely for multitasking and "intuition." These two talents may depend upon the ability of the two hemispheres to communicate particularly efficiently, which may be something female brains are specialized to do. Men seem to have more "lateralized" brain function; for a number of tasks they rely somewhat more on one hemisphere than the other.

Differences in Brain Function

Researchers have also discovered a number of behaviors, abilities, or tendencies in which one sex, on average, scored higher than the other. All are tasks carried out by our brains. (Remember that the curves for the sexes overlap—there is often more difference between individual boys and girls, individual men and women, than there is between the two sexes). Fisher discusses many of these features, suggesting why evolution may have favored that skill in one sex or the other:

- Men tolerate acute pain better.
- Women tolerate long-term discomfort better.
- Women are better able to decipher facial expressions.
- Women are more capable at multi-tasking.
- Women are more inclined to long-term planning.
- Men are more inclined to focus tightly on a problem.
- Men exhibit more emotional control.
- Women have better intuitional judgment.
- Men are more likely to take risks.

The cutting edge on the study of brain function has gone hightech. Volunteers are asked to perform tasks—let's say something verbal—and they are studied with either a PET scanner or an MRI scanner. These are live-brain tests.

PET stands for positron emission tomography. A solution of sugar marked with a radioactive isotope is injected into the volunteer, the person is asked to perform the task, and then the investigator measures where in the brain the radioactive isotope shows up. The rationale is that cells use sugar for energy when they work. If cells start to work a bit harder in an area of the brain devoted to the specified task, the cells in that area will consume more sugar. The scanner registers and indicates the area of the brain involved. These live-brain studies have, for example, shown different patterns of activation between men and women doing certain word tests or math/spatial tests.

Magnetic resonance imaging (MRI) involves creating a magnetic field around the head that induces the protons in hydrogen atoms in cells to align along the same axis. When a radio frequency pulse (RF pulse) is directed to a specific area, it causes some protons to line up slightly differently, and then when the RF is turned off, the protons realign. As they realign, they release energy in a signal that can be detected and sent to a computer. The computer generates a precise picture of the tissue.

For example, Deborah Blum describes the work of Sally and Bennett Shaywitz, who looked at gender differences and language processing. They asked their subjects to do a rhyming task while under an MRI scanner. In most men, as they matched words with appropriate rhymes (cake, bake), a small center called the inferior frontal gyrus (behind the eyebrow) lit up only on the left side. For women, the tendency was for this region to light up in both hemispheres.

Studies on Infants and Cross-cultural Studies of Children

We are barely at the beginning of the age of exploring this extraordinary inner world of the mind, and we will surely find many more male/female differences. Studies involving infants will be critical

Women, Power, and the Biology of Peace

Also important are cross-cultural studies looking at gender differences in behavior in infants and young children. If we detect differences in infants, very young children, and across cultures, we secure strong evidence that the differences are the result of nature rather than nurture.

Note, for example, that we can't know whether the structural brain differences I described earlier are the result of the genes directing the brains' construction, or rather that the brains are anatomically different in adults because of a lifetime of learning. Learning affects the brain, and the anatomical studies referred to above were done on the brains of deceased adults.

Similarly, the live-brain function studies described above were also done on adults who, as Blum emphasizes in *Sex On The Brain,* had been subjected to a lifetime of learning. What we need are similar PET and MRI studies involving infants. Given current technology, where the subject must lie still for a long period in a strange contraption, restless infants don't make ideal subjects, but some progress is still being made.

A Field Guide to Boys and Girls by Susan Gilbert, a fine book for parents, describes just how early in time some major sex differences in behavior begin to appear, as does Blum in *Sex on the Brain*

Note once again that the differences between genders are usually not large. One of the biggest differences, for example, is that boys, cross-culturally, engage in more rough and tumble play than girls do. They are more likely to pummel, wrestle, and pretend-fight. But only a small percent of the boys—15-20% in one study cited by Gilbert—score higher than did any girls. Most boys' and girls' scores overlap.

These studies do show, however, that materials for building an adult are not exactly the same in populations of young males and females. Some examples taken from Gilbert:

- The INAH-3, a tiny pin-prick-size cluster of cells is the same size in male and female babies but begins to enlarge in boys when

they are about ten. The implication is that the genetically timed increase in testosterone secretion associated with puberty causes the changes in boys. The cluster has one half to three times more nerve cells in adult men than women, and it is thought to be involved in regulating sexual desire.
- The two brain hemispheres develop at different rates in girls and boys. The left, the one most involved in language processing, develops more quickly in girls. The right, the side critical to spatial tasks, develops more quickly in boys.
- Within hours of delivery, girls, on average, seem more social than boys in that they maintain eye contact longer with people and are more responsive to other people and to sounds.
- Boys cry more, become more easily upset, and stay upset longer, on average, than girls.
- Girls' fine motor skills develop, on average, faster than boys'.

On average:

- Girls talk earlier than boys.
- Girls develop emotional or impulse control sooner than boys.
- Boys are more physically aggressive than girls.
- Girls are more verbally aggressive in the form of gossip or fighting words.
- Boys are more openly and physically involved in establishing dominance, while girls prefer to "get along" with a network, a friend, or a few friends, and to establish dominance by subtle means.

Here, taken slightly modified from Debra Tannen's *The Argument Culture,* is a description of a play session that, while it involved older students, typifies what one sees even with young children:

Two boys and a girl who were friends were playing a game of blocks. Each had built a structure, a unique design. Suddenly, one boy threw a block at the other boy's structure to knock it over. The second boy retaliated by throwing a block at the first boy's structure. The first boy then threw a block at the girl's. She put her arms around her building to shield it from flying blocks. The two boys happily destroyed each other's buildings but couldn't get hers because they didn't want to hit her with the blocks. A third boy came over and asked her why she didn't throw blocks back, and she said she didn't like to play that way and didn't find it fun.

As Tannen says, it's not that boys are insensitive and mean. It's a kind of game for the boys. It was fun. Note that the girl's reaction was not to flee, but to defend her building. I discuss later the powerful inclination women have for defense (see **Women as Warriors**).

Blum describes the work of Martin Hoffman who studied the emotional responses of day-old infants to various sounds: animal calls, the weird droning voice of a computer, and babies crying. The strongest response of these day-old infants was to the sounds of human crying. And it was the *female* infants who reacted most strongly to the sounds of human distress. Certainly in these cases, learning cannot be involved.

It is culture—in the form of parents, siblings, friends, and the social environment at large—that takes these overlapping yet different beginning materials and shapes them. We then end up with little boys who grow into men having the male characteristics expected by their culture, and little girls who grow into women having the expected female characteristics.

For example, Gilbert cites studies that show that parents do a variety of things that encourage girls to speak and discourage boys from doing so, and that parents have many more face-to-face "conversations" with infant daughters than sons. Peers are also critical. One study looked at the popularity of children in fourth to sixth grade. Boys who fought back were popular. Girls who fought back weren't.

The Outer Boundaries of Human Nature

The extraordinary flexibility of human behavior and the critical importance of culture in shaping our behavior are undeniable. **But it is equally true that we cannot live contrary to our nature.**

We cannot, for example, hope to eliminate the human penchant for creating dominance hierarchies and for being keenly aware of status. To propose such a thing is pointless folly. There are no human societies where the sense of rank or status is absent, even if that be found only within the families of those societies. In Christopher Boehm's wide-ranging study of "egalitarian" societies worldwide, *Hierarchy in the Forest,* he reports that sensitivity to the urge to rise in rank is acute among egalitarian people, and that egalitarian societies actually must work very hard, using all sorts of traditions and customs, to make certain that the group's members remain "equal." They work to make sure that no one seeks or achieves higher rank than anyone else. He describes many methods they use to exercise control, including making fun of anyone who even begins to hint that he or she is somehow "better."

So what sometimes does work is for societies to build traditions, laws, and customs to shape and limit a particular human penchant. One of the main goals of liberal democracies, for example, is to moderate the urge to rise in status to the point of dominating all others.

Consider another example of how our nature limits us. Consider a social system based on the notion that each person will work but the greater portion of the profit from his or her labor—say 60-70%—will be given to other people who work very little but need it more. Unless these laborers get something back that they value very highly indeed, this system is ultimately doomed. Witness the many tax revolts in history, the stunning demise of Russian communism, and the evolution of Chinese communism to capitalism.

Another example. You might convince goodly numbers of the members of a society to allow children from impoverished, dangerous neighborhoods to be bussed into their own, safe neighborhood to attend school—providing you convince the adults that such an effort serves some very great good. But you would never convince any significant number of people to bus their children into an unsafe neighborhood, no matter how hard you might try or how worthy your cause.

To attempt any of the above or anything else that is contrary to our nature, perhaps thinking we can bring it off through education or some sort of social engineering, is to spit into the wind. If it's contrary to our nature, it will ultimately be unstable. **At some point we reach an outer boundary where our innate nature absolutely limits what is possible.**

We cannot eliminate the penchant to band together in an aggressive mood that has the potential to escalate into battle. Nor can we eliminate the penchant to make nice and make peace. We need to learn how to control and benefit from both tendencies, to learn how to make the best of what we are by nature.

The trick is to know the outer boundaries. Then anything that lies within that wide scope is possible if we choose it and foster it. The challenge becomes a matter of creating the conditions that favor what we desire.

Summary of the Central Hypothesis of Women, Power, and the Biology of Peace

My view, shared with many others and often felt to be self evident, is that a tendency for males to band together and be easily roused to an aggressive group effort is innate. Whether to achieve dominance, hunt for food, or protect the group, it's in our bones and being. Later we'll consider how this tendency is magnified in warrior cultures while in peaceful societies, it is suppressed and controlled—but is still there.

Males encouraged to behave these ways do so because the behavior is reinforcing: exciting, thrilling, challenging, riveting.

Women, Power, and the Biology of Peace

Chris Hedges, in *War Is a Force That Gives Us Meaning*, powerfully describes this effect in war, likening it to drug addiction. Evolution has made such bonding and expression of ferocity a pleasure because it enhanced male reproductive success. It facilitates hunting and defense of one's social group. In the right context, such as losing—or even winning—a soccer match, men erupt into this behavior, even if it results in havoc. This is overwhelmingly a male inclination. If there is a riot in the streets or a brawl in the bar, it will be rare that the majority of participants are female.

The other half of the hypothesis is that females, sometimes even many females, can be similarly roused to aggression, and they can also find bonding together for a common cause exciting and thrilling. They can even be so roused by anger that they become frighteningly aggressive, even vicious (see **Defense vs. Offense** below). But it is much harder to rouse great numbers of women to this state of aggression and harder still to keep them there because, on average, women find greater reinforcement in an environment that is not in turmoil. Because of genetic inclinations that are as deeply rooted as the bonding-for-aggression inclinations of men, most women would prefer to make or keep the peace, the sooner the better.

Section II – A Powerful, Creative Civilization without War – Is That Possible?

> .... some contemporary feminists assert that most prior history was the history of conflicts among "patriarchal" societies, but that "matriarchal" societies, more consensual, nurturing, and prone to peace, constitute a viable alternative. This cannot be demonstrated on the basis of empirical fact, since there are no existing examples of matriarchal societies. And yet, the possibility of their future existence cannot be ruled out, if the feminist understanding of the possibilities for the liberation of the female side of the human personality proves to be correct. And if it is so, then we clearly have not reached the end of history."
>
>   ❧ Francis Fukuyama
>   ❧ *The End of History and the Last Man*

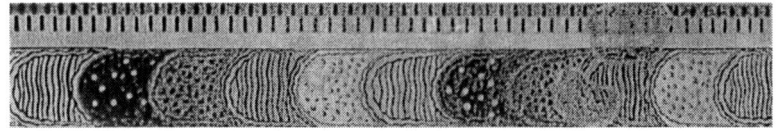

The Keftian Way

*I*s war a necessary evil, the critical fuel for advances in knowledge and technology? Not a few philosophers have argued that it is. Was there ever a time when women ran or had an equal influence in a state-level civilization? If the answer is *yes*, what did such a society look like? Did it achieve sophistication without war?

All evidence to date indicates that the Minoans represent a rare, if not unique, moment in history showing us one view of how civilized living might have looked if women had been participants in matters of state—if women had been running things, or at least had had a share in running things and in a society without war.

A word about the name Minoan. When Sir Arthur Evans discovered the ruins at Knossos, he thought he had discovered the palace of Minos, the mythical Greek king. Hence the name, Minoan. But as I point out below, there is no evidence these people had a king. I consider this name a misnomer, and so use the name *Keftian*, which comes from their Egyptian contemporaries. Painted on the wall of an Egyptian tomb are men dressed in what is clearly Cretan garb who appear to be bringing gifts to the pharaoh. An inscription says they are the "ambassadors from Keftiu." Linguists suggest still other similar names, for example Kaptares. Whatever their true name, the name "Minoan" is an accident of history.

Comparing State-Level Civilizations

Giving women the vote in modern democracies—an event that in the United States happened only roughly eighty years ago—may well prove to have been a pivotal step in one of the single biggest revolutions in world history—an astonishingly quiet revolution, but profound. Before this time, with perhaps the single exception of the Keftians, women had never had the vote or a voice in state-level civilizations. While they may have been influential, even powerful, in their home or their family sphere, for millennia the decisions in state-level societies about running the state and going to war have been made virtually exclusively by men.

This is not to say that women in many tribal and community-based cultures have not wielded power. For example, women of the Iroquois Nation in North America were highly influential. They even exercised the vote in the Iroquois version of democracy. (See also Fry, D., 2006, 2007.)

There have been in the past and still are societies where women hold power positions equal or near-equal to men (for examples see Sanday, P., 1981). In Sweden in 2007, for example, 47.3 % of members of the congress were women. Most such cultures, however, do not display the level of social organization that anthropologists or historians would recognize as a state-level society.

A state-level society is, first of all, markedly hierarchical: it shows an impressive proliferation of social classes. In addition, common techniques for making pottery or other material artifacts extend across a wide region. A strong central authority also is in place that has the ability to marshal massive resources of materials and labor. In the past, this typically resulted in, for one thing, the construction of impressive architectural structures executed in stone. Think of the Egyptian pyramids, the Hanging Gardens of Babylon, the Aztec temples, the Inca's Machu Picchu, and the Great Wall of China. The Keftian complex at Knossos is evidence of this level of social organization.

So when I suggest that the Keftians appear to be unique, it is to other such state-level societies that I'm comparing them. In the history of humanity, no other civilizations that we know about achieved state-level without warfare. It is for this reason that a close look at the Keftians is particularly instructive.

The Keftians – Who, When, Where

Crete was the center of the Keftian culture. Additionally, ruins from the same Bronze Age time period on the island of Santorini show strong Keftian influence. Santorini lies roughly seventy miles north of Crete. Dating this period of history in the Mediterranean is still difficult, but the time is roughly 1650 – 1450 BCE.

Santorini once had a substantial, active volcano at its heart, and around 1628 BCE, a date in which we have much more confidence since the fallout can be radioactively dated, the volcano exploded. This was an event ten times bigger than Indonesia's Krakatoa and easily sixty to a hundred times bigger than the American Mt. St. Helens. Because the 1650-1450 BCE dates, based mostly on comparisons of pottery styles from different periods, are so uncertain, and some experts think could easily be too late by a hundred or more years, various scholars have proposed this explosion as a possible cause of the Keftian decline. It so weakened them, the theory goes, that forces from the mainland, eager to acquire the Keftian's wealth and the strategic advantage of their island's central location on sea lanes, were able to take over. In fact, the cause of the shift from the Minoan period to the Mycenaean period that followed remains a mystery.

The Keftians had a written language, Linear A, but it hasn't been translated, and so we are greatly limited in our knowledge of them. We have no written descriptions of their lives or social system or religion. We can only recreate their world based on artifacts they left behind, on our knowledge of surrounding and subsequent history and mythology and on our understanding of human nature. What follows are the facts and rationale used in my reconstruction in the novel wherever that reconstruction relates to the subject of peace and war or the possible power of women in this exceptional culture.

Matriarchy and the Use of Power

Matriarchy?

There is no reason in the archeological evidence or in historical precedent to think the Keftians might have been a matriarchy. The suffix -*archy* has to do with ruling. We've had patriarchies. We've had oligarchies. But there is no documented case in history, including the history of tribal cultures, of a matriarchy—a society in which women ruled and men were ruled over. Not one example where women controlled all of their society's levers of social power.

We have many examples of cultures where women are highly important (see Matrilocality below), but to my knowledge, in all such societies, men also have a share in community decisions. Such cultures can only be called Matriarchal by redefining (weakening) the word, which undermines its usefulness. And while history records many extraordinary women who, in patriarchal state-level societies, rose against the odds to positions of high power, those women stand as exceptions that prove the rule.

"This extraordinary matriarchy." That's how my publisher wanted me to promote my work of fiction. Yet even as I was wrangling with him, saying I didn't think they were a matriarchy and I didn't depict them as one, I realized that -*archy* is a very male thing. That's how he, a male, instinctively interpreted the situation I had portrayed. Because Keftian artifacts portray no male rulers and, in fact, because central figures are typically female, I envisioned a culture where the final decisions in state matters were made and voiced by a woman, the High Priestess, who spoke for their chief divinity, a goddess.

Since placing a woman in such high position is an unusual and therefore attention-catching feature, the superficial label might be "matriarchy." But that wouldn't make it a matriarchy. That my publisher would want to call it one illustrates the distance, semantic and otherwise, we need to travel to avoid misunderstanding.

Given that there is no historical precedent for matriarchy, I specifically included in the novel many men who have positions of social authority: the heroine's vizier; her principal mentor; the head of her navy; the head of the city council; the head of the Bull Leaping Academy. This would not be true in a matriarchy. To be a matriarchy it would be as in a patriarchy but reversed: there might be a rare, extraordinary man now and then who would gain a position of public power, but such men would be exceptions. Women would run or head virtually everything.

Use of Power – Making Decisions for the Community

In hunter-gatherer cultures where women *are* community decision-makers, or in community-based societies where women enjoy critical social influence, community power is usually not centralized but spread out so that both men and women participate in decision-making. There is an approach to male/female balance. One sex does not make all decisions. Instead, men typically decide some issues, women decide others.

Consider the Goba of the Zambezi. According to Chet Lancaster, they are a "women-centered" culture. Some call them matriarchal. Nevertheless, men hold most political offices and men make decisions about the care of and commerce in cattle. Women make decisions about the care of the critical gardens and decide whether grain resources can be spared for making much-valued beer.

In small societies where women's views carry weight, decisions on important issues may require consultation and agreement within the entire group, including all the women. In some cultures, the shaman may be a man for example, and he may decide matters of belief, while the decision about when the group should break camp to move to a summer or winter quarter may be left to a women's council. In some larger communities, two groups, amen's council and a women's council, may consult separately and then negotiate together and reach agreement before any major group action is taken.

While patriarchy in some form is characteristic of many tribal cultures, in his book *Hierarchy in the Forest, The Evolution of Egalitarian Behavior,* Christopher Boehm focuses particularly on tribes and bands that are egalitarian. He describes how, by virtue of women's strong exercise of what he calls "moral authority," women in these egalitarian hunter-gatherer cultures share forcefully in regulating male behavior. Ridicule is one tool for social control. Men and women alike make pointed fun of anyone who slips out of line. Should a hunter bring home a particularly fine gazelle and succumb to the temptation to brag, a woman may comment gleefully that, "It's such a shame that most of your catches are so puny." The society also uses the power of shunning or, in serious cases, ostracism, to punish infractions by what Boehm calls "upstart" males.

Ember and Ember describe the Iroquois as follows: "Among the Iroquois of North America, women had control over resources and a great deal of influence. But men held political office, not women. The highest political body among the League of the Iroquois (comprised of five different tribal groups) was a council of fifty male chiefs. The women could not serve on the council, but they could nominate, elect, and impeach their male representatives. Women also could decide between life or death for prisoners of war, they could forbid the men of their households to go to war, and they could intervene to bring about peace." Again, the pattern in this culture with power-holding women was that social power was not highly centralized nor entirely in the hands of one sex.

How Women Use Power

As Boehm's work indicates, in egalitarian hunter-gatherer groups, a male urge to rise in status is restrained by customs and social conventions. When unrestrained, however, human males form dominance relationships that result in hierarchies of power in which position in the hierarchy is highly important to each man and power is primarily exercised by fiat from the top down the chain. Boehm makes the importance of social restraint clear by focusing on so-called egalitarian societies and showing how hard they work to curb this male inclination.

Human females also establish hierarchies and protect their status. There should be no doubt. Women are as interested in power as are men, clearly explored by Hrdy in *Mother Nature*.

But there are notable differences in how women who acquire power exercise it and for what goals. In *The First Sex,* Fisher argues that when possessing power and confronted with choices, women are *in general* more inclined to network and listen to many voices to find a win-win solution, a term which originated in game theory.

Win-win resolution requires cooperation between the parties in disagreement rather than a heads-on competition, winner-take-all mentality. A comparable term for win-win conflict resolution is "mutual gains bargaining." The essence of the process lies in keeping all parties reasonably satisfied. Each may not get everything desired, but they get much of what they want and in fact need. This avoids the pitfall of slipping into conflicts and retaliations where, in the end, no one wins (lose-lose).

Debra Tannen's chapter on "Boys Will Be Boys, Gender and Opposition" highlights many of the same points. She describes, for example, some of the research of linguist Amy Sheldon, who compared boys and girls in conflict over toys and how the two sexes resolved the conflicts. Tannen sums up the studies as showing that, "...girls appear less forceful only if you take the boys' behavior as the norm. If you look at the girls on their own terms, they are forceful and assertive in a different (less overtly physical) way. They use the force of their wills to balance their needs with the needs of others."

According to Fisher, as described in *The First Sex,* women also are more prospicient, more inclined to think long-term, to anticipate problems within the community (or business or family) and to think and plan ahead. They then use their power to avoid or mitigate them. Men also think long-term, but Fisher cites evidence that women more *habitually* do so, as if always looking to anticipate future needs and difficulties so that these can be met or resolved with minimal or no conflict.

How individual men or women use power is not in question here. There are always individuals who don't fit the "pattern" for their sex: a woman who is extremely assertive, a man who is painfully retiring, women who may be more competitive than any of the men in their group, and a few men in a group who may be uninterested in competition in any form. Nevertheless, the *general* difference in male and female ways of exercising power makes biological sense. This is because over the long run, when individuals must interact repeatedly, **win-win conflict resolution tends to facilitate a more stable social milieu, an important female priority.** A win-lose approach tends to produce winners and losers— and a retaliatory mentality.

Who's Your Mother? Where Do You Live?

While it's highly unlikely that the Keftians were a matriarchy, what may very well have been true for them is that they were matrilineal and matrilocal.

Matrilineality

Keeping track of kinship is a pervasive human preoccupation. We are fascinated by who is related to whom, and we find that family ties are often critical to our success. And the numbers and kinds of relationships people can pay attention to are mind-boggling. To study kinship systems across many cultures can be daunting. In simplest terms, though, if parentage is traced through the father, it is patrilineal. If traced through the mother, it is matrilineal.

Even in a number of strongly patriarchal societies, lineage is traced through the mother's line due to the straightforward biological fact that at birth, we always know who is the mother of a child. But it is far from easy to be certain who the father is.

From a biological perspective, it's important that the resources an individual controls are given to one's own offspring (see *Mother Nature*). One can gain status by sharing excess resources with others or by controlling resources and doling them out to others. But one's highest evolutionary priority is to one's own children. Recognizing one's own children is no problem for a mother—but it's a big problem for a father. If a man is to ensure that his resources go to his offspring, it is important for him to know which of a woman's children belong to him.

In the modern world, medical testing makes paternity theoretically easy to determine, but in the past in a society where women were free, this goal was virtually impossible for men to achieve. And a prime reason males have had great difficulty determining whether they fathered a particular child has to do with an odd feature of human biology—"hidden ovulation."

Human females are unusual among primates. Not only can they and will they have sex at any time they choose during their menstrual cycle—that is, they are "continually receptive" (most other female primates are like most mammals in that they "come into heat")—human females do not signal the time of their greatest fertility in any outward manner. Ovulation is "hidden."

Consider chimpanzees. When a female chimpanzee comes into heat, her sexual parts swell visibly, prominently announcing her fertile condition. If at this time, a male chimp remains with her and allows no other males but himself to have mating access to her, he is assured—or pretty much so—that her offspring are his.

(He must, of course, occasionally sleep, or he may at some moment become distracted even in this situation, so he can't have 100% confidence.)

But in humans, evolution favored the hiding of a woman's fertile period. This makes paternity assurance extremely problematical for human males. (I return to this odd condition below when comparing humans, chimpanzees, and bonobos.)

Hidden ovulation and continuous receptivity mean that only in extremely strong patriarchies, where the lives of women are tightly regulated, can males be assured that they have fathered a given child. Indeed, such practices as female sequestration (restriction to a harem or the home) and infundibulation (removal of the clitoris then sewing together the labia to minimize the opening to the vagina thus preventing sexual pleasure) are radical attempts in some patriarchal societies to insure that the mother's child actually belongs to her husband (despite whatever social or cultural reasons may be offered to explain the behavior).

Although matrilineality is often found in societies where women have considerable power, if we look across many cultures, matrilineality is not strongly correlated with empowerment of women. In patriarchal cultures, it's merely a way to keep track of parentage, although through the mother's line, with sons being the offspring that inherit wealth and power.

Matrilocality

The second term, however, often is associated with female empowerment. The term "matrilocal" applies to marriage customs. Specifically, it describes one way of resolving the question of residence after a couple complete their wedding vows.

In societies living at low densities and widely spread out, the pair may move away from both families to begin their own "homestead." In most societies, though, one member of the couple must leave his or her family and go to the home or at least the village or town of the other spouse. They move to where that spouse's family holds its resources—perhaps a farm, or plot of garden, or fishing rights. **And the spouse that moves loses power.** They leave behind their relatives and friends—their allies. When the woman joins her husband and his kin, the system is patrilocal, and when he leaves his family and moves in with hers, it is matrilocal.

In a matrilocal society, family property is handed down through the mother's line, from mothers to daughters. (In a minority of cases, a woman's brother makes all property decisions, so the woman owns the resources in name only). The husband typically comes into a situation where the matriarch—and here the word is very appropriate—runs the family, and he contributes his labor to the efforts of his wife's family. If the marriage doesn't go well, there may be a divorce—he usually returns to his family—but he is the one who leaves while the wife stays with her family, still supported and assured of resources for herself and her children.

In societies where women actually control the resources, matri-locality does have a strong correlation with women being powerful. This is for the obvious reason that women are in control of vital resources. In biology—in life—resources are the main name of the power game. For humans there are many paths to power—one can climb the status ladder by being a great shaman or artist, warrior or hunter—but he or she who controls vital resources always has power.

I therefore depicted the Keftians as tracing their lineage and holding and passing their family resources through the mother's line.

Art and Artifacts

If you were presented with the remains of a long dead world and had no written records about its people, where would you begin to try to reconstruct their lives? Would it not have to be with their art and their artifacts? Our knowledge of Keftian society is severely limited. What we think we know can only be inferred from the

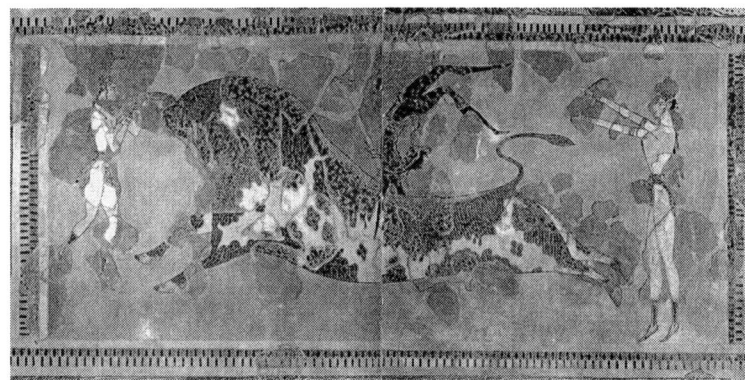

Figure 1: The Bull Leapers

art and artifacts that survived the millennia that separate us from them, artifacts recovered and restored by Arthur Evans and the archaeologists that followed him.

Women At Least Equal To Men In Influence

What do these artifacts suggest about the relative power position of Keftian men and women in this rare, perhaps unique, state-level society that appears not to have suffered the blight of wars?

1. In Keftian Art, Women Are Prominent

The Bull Leapers is a fresco well known to students of art history. It was my first introduction to these extraordinary people decades ago when, as an undergraduate, I took a class in ancient history.

Our professor had explained that the bull was an important cultural symbol, probably religious in nature. The fresco does depict a magnificent bull along with three human figures. We know that two of the three figures are female because the Keftians followed the same artistic convention used by their Egyptian contemporaries: they painted female bodies light and male bodies darker. The figures also have breasts.

What is noteworthy is not that some women were depicted. What is important is that women were central to whatever socially or

Figure 2: The Procession

religiously significant action is immortalized here. They were important to the very meaning of the event.

I vividly remember being amazed. The phrase "women's liberation movement" lay quite a number of years into the American future. American women were still expected to spend their time almost exclusively tending hearth and home.

2. Their Chief Divinity was Female

The most important deity they worshipped was a goddess. This is highly suggestive as one piece of the whole picture of how they felt about women as it implies deference. But it certainly isn't definitive; many societies or communities that have worshipped goddesses have at the same time treated women abominably.

The goddess's name was Potnia, which translates to The Lady. We know this because Linear B, a related language, a form of early Greek, has been translated and refers to this goddess. In ancient cultures, goddesses were often prevalent and powerful along with gods, but the Keftians are uncommon in that the **chief** divinity in their pantheon was not a god, but a goddess.

3. The Central Or Most Prominent Figures in Mixed Social Scenes are Most Commonly Female

Many examples of female prominence in social imagery are found on vases, seal stones, and other artifacts. I illustrate with the famous fresco, **The Procession.**

The Procession is a large art piece on the walls of a great, long corridor in the ruins of Knossos. The many human figures are almost life-size, and there are estimated to be roughly a hundred to perhaps two hundred of them.

The figures converge from the left and right onto a central figure—painted white. A female! Perhaps a representation of a high priestess. Perhaps a representation of the goddess.

She does not appear to be a Queen as she is neither larger than the other figures nor elevated over them, nor are the figures bowing to her or kneeling. Whatever the figure represents, the fresco makes a female its central figure.

Other notable fresco examples are **Akrotiri Town** and the **Mixed Audience**. In the Akrotiri "town" scene, numerous human figures are engaged in various activities. If all are examined closely for size, the largest are three women: one alone on a balcony and two women together on another balcony.

The Mixed Audience shows a large crowd watching some event. One interesting feature is that the men and women are not mixed together but are in single-sex groups. What is significant to this point on the power of women, however, is that women are present in what appears to be an equal number to men, and in several places they are depicted prominently in the foreground.

It is also notable in Keftian art that one never finds the extreme sexual imbalance found in many impressive Egyptian pieces where the male is a huge figure and the female tiny. Moreover, scenes that appear to be religious show both men and women in featured positions. One sex is not systematically relegated to the background or to only rare occurrence. Keftian art considered as a whole conveys some sense of gender balance, but at the same time there is a notable preference for women.

4. No Depictions of a King

Although negative evidence (lack of evidence) cannot prove anything, absence is sometimes highly suggestive. On seal stones and other objects, we find occasional depictions of a male that appear to be representations of a god, but Keftian art has no depictions of a king performing "kingly" acts such as sitting on a throne, riding in a chariot, lording over subjects, or addressing the divinity. This is notable because kings are often the central figures in a culture's larger art pieces; indeed, kings are usually extraordinarily eager to have themselves immortalized in art.

The closest thing to such an artifact is this fresco called **The Prince**.

Like The Procession, this fresco is large, almost life-sized. It portrays

Figure 3: The Prince

what appears to be a young man (no breasts—but oddly the body is light-colored). He stands in a field of plants. Butterflies are also present, and his pose is a bit peculiar.

Recall that Sir Arthur Evans believed he had discovered the palace of the mythical Minos. As a result, while he and his team of restorers carried out their labors, they were looking for evidence of a king. This good-sized figure was the closest they came.

Note that what most gives the young man a regal bearing is the fancy, plumed crown or headdress. Note also that **the fancy headdress was not found in the same room.** It was found amid the rubble of another room. Here was a clearly imposing headdress, and to give their reconstruction of Knossos life, the restorers had to decide who might have worn this magnificent piece. If there must have been a king, then surely this must be him, they may have thought, hence the name, "The Prince."

In reality we have no idea who or what the figure is. It could have been their most famous bull leaper. Perhaps it was a depiction of an annual god that was ceremonially married to the goddess as her consort each spring. Even perhaps the artist's vision of a hermaphroditic world (no breasts, light body color) that combined the best of both men and women.

The point is that while there are many depictions of women in central or important positions in Keftian art, there are few of men, and none resembling a king.

A Sophisticated Culture

What else do the artifacts tell us? It quickly becomes evident, when one visits the museums or studies photographs, that these people were, early on, wonderfully sophisticated. This is roughly 1600 – 1400 BCE. The classical Greeks lay some thousand years into the future. The time of Christ would wait some 1,600 years for its time on the world's stage. And while the rest of Europe was at this time rustic, the Keftians had:

Great Architecture – Figure 4 is an artist's representation of what Evans called the Palace of King Minos but what might just as plausibly have been the Temple of the Great Goddess. To gain some perspective, consider that a later palace on the Greek mainland at a town called Pylos was built by the warrior culture that replaced the Keftians, the Mycenaeans. In Homer's Iliad, Pylos was said to be the site of the magnificent Palace of King Nestor. Well, Nestor's entire magnificent palace would fit nicely into the great Central Court of the Knossos complex.

At that Bronze Age time, this structure would have evoked stunned awe in Europe. Some sections stand six stories high; thousands of people could have worked within its rooms, gardens, and courts. Its construction would have required vast resources in terms of materials and human labor and is one of our strongest proofs that this was indeed a state-level civilization. At the height of this culture, smaller but similarly designed structures were also constructed at other Cretan sites, such as Phaestos, Gournia, and Mallia.

Women, Power, and the Biology of Peace

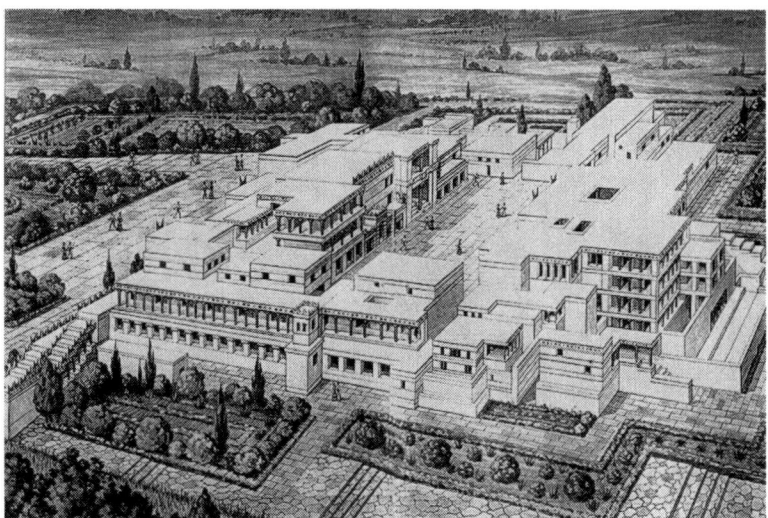

Figure 4: Temple at Knossos

Paved Roads – At the extreme upper left corner of the Knossos complex, two figures are descending a flight of stairs. Those stairs lead down to the beginning of a paved road that stretched roughly twenty-seven miles from Knossos to its main seaport, Amnissos. The first paved roads in Europe are on Crete. It seems these fastidious people weren't fond of mud and dust.

Flush Toilets – Perhaps my favorite discovery, because it made me laugh out loud, was to learn that their fancier buildings had not only running water but also indoor flush toilets.

Underground Drains – Again, their fastidiousness is expressed in the invention of cleverly designed underground drains, and their sophistication in the construction of at least one aqueduct.

Elegant, Joyful Art – Finally, we have their art. Art is a mirror of a culture. It doesn't, however, depict everything a people do. For example, we may be fascinated by such exceptions as the famous brothel frescoes of Pompeii and some of the more graphic depictions on Greek vases, but many cultures produce little art that gives

Figure 5: The Swallows

insight into their intimate sexual habits. A culture's art is especially unlikely to depict things they weren't proud of.

But it certainly does depict what they value. Keftian art is often lively and elegant with a joyful spirit and great reverence for nature. Figures 5 & 6 are small sections of nature scenes that decorated walls.

Figures 7-9 (page 67), **The Girl From Akrotiri, The Girl With Shaved Head**, and the men on **The Harvester Vase**, illustrate another feature of Keftian art. Whenever the Keftians depicted facial expressions, the subjects often wear a grin or knowing smile.

Nothing in Keftian art is heavy, gloomy, or threatening. Rather it shows a sense of fun or joy, and in many scenes of dancing, what appears to be religious ecstasy.

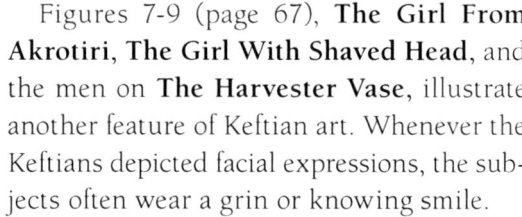
Figure 6: The Bluebird

Peace

What is most important with respect to warfare is what the artifacts do not say. Some very provocative things are missing from the traces the millennia did not erase. This culture persisted for several hundred years, yet there is **no convincing evidence of warfare on the Crete of the Keftian/Minoan period.**

Among academics, this apparent social stability is highly controversial. If it's true, the Keftians may be the only people to have reached state-level without engaging in internal and external wars.

Figure 7: Girl from Akrotiri

Figure 8: Girl with shaved head

Figure 9: The Harvester Vase (selection)

Recently, the Caral and Harappa have emerged as other possibilities. This is what makes the Keftians important, because **their existence suggests that war is not an unavoidable result of, nor is it requisite for, the development of complex, and sophisticated societies.**

At the peak of their influence, the Keftians were highly sophisticated, surely sophisticated enough to know they needed a navy with armed marines—primarily to combat piracy on their critical trade routes. Later Greek tradition said that the people on Crete had a powerful navy that ruled the sea. But they do not appear to have engaged in the internal wars that were, for example, so typical hundreds of years later of the Greek city-states on the mainland.

Unfortunately, this is a distant period of history and a part of the world with few written records, and Linear A has not been deciphered. A second reason this peace hypothesis is controversial is because it is based on negative evidence. We have no written records to confirm or disprove the thesis, neither Keftian writing nor accounts of their contemporaries. Without positive evidence of some kind, such as written records, we may never have certainty about the question of enduring peace on Keftian Crete. But we can consider the nature of the negative evidence, and then make assessments of the provocative possibilities.

Crete is a large island—roughly 150 miles long and 65 miles wide—long and narrow. At the peak of Keftian culture, hundreds of towns and at least six to seven large cities dotted the landscape.

- None of those cities or towns was fortified, as if they had no need to defend against each other. Lack of city fortification is a particularly striking absence. While the Keftians often selected building sites with good views of the surrounding countryside—they did love the natural world—the sites were not perched on top of clearly defendable positions.
- No excavations to date reveal large weapons caches or places where people were fashioning weapons for defense or aggression. One can always argue that raiders have long since found such caches and the weapons and the remains from constructing them have been taken away. But while we occasionally find such sites associated with other cultures that engaged in war, we find none on Keftian Crete.
- Keftian art has few or no depictions of violence. Even exciting depictions of engagements with bulls usually avoid anyone being hurt, human or bull. Certainly there are no depictions of killing or subjugation or siege. The

one possible exception is a fresco not actually from Crete but from Akrotiri on Santorini. The scene appears to be a battle at sea. Also at Akrotiri, a fresco depicts men with shields and spears, perhaps a contingent of marines returning home from sea duty. But no such depictions are found on Keftian Crete. There is, in short, no evidence of veneration or celebration of war or conquest.

- Collapsed and burned Keftian buildings do show signs of destruction that might be attributed to warfare or revolt. But the destruction can just as plausibly be attributed to terrible earthquakes and subsequent fires. Keftians certainly were plagued by serious quakes, conditions well described in *The Search for Atlantis* by Charles Pellegrino and *The Troubled Island* by Jan Driessen and Colin McDonald.
- Weapons such as swords or spears are rarely found in burials, even those of men. That inclusion of war weapons in burials was common in other nearby cultures of the time is additional negative evidence that war and its trappings were not central to Keftian culture.
- We do find evidence on Crete of outposts scattered here and there over the landscape. Some investigators have described these as fortifications because they have stone walls, or what appears to be a base for a stone wall. Some investigators, expecting and perhaps looking for signs of warfare (much as Evans was looking for signs of a king), have called these watchtowers. They argue that from these locations, men watched for signs of approaching invaders. Since the sites don't commonly appear to face the sea, the assumption is further made that the anticipated invaders were from Crete itself, not abroad. But many more studies will be required before we can honestly say what these structures were. They may have been mountain sanctuaries, shrines, or retreats for religious or other purposes. They may be no more than retaining walls, or walls of agricultural terraces, or to enclose sheep. They may even have

been resting places for caravans or for messengers carrying communications between the cities. Since no weapons have been found associated with them, to conclude that they indicate internal warfare seems wildly premature.

If Keftians were as peaceful as Keftian artifacts found to date indicate, it **would prove that something other than living in complex groups is the cause of war.** It would prove that to find the causes of armed conflict, we must look elsewhere. If true, it also offers the profound hope that through the increasing participation of women in the affairs of the world, we maybe able to free ourselves from the specter of repeated wars.

Why Only The Keftians?

Six Necessary Conditions

After contemplating the Keftian case, I suggest that to reach state-level organization without resorting to consolidation through war, at least six factors—six "necessary conditions"—must have been present. A consideration of these conditions sheds light not only on why we likely have had only one such culture in all of history, but also on the causes of war. To the extent that we can understand the likely sources of the Keftian's success, we may learn more about the conditions necessary for social stability of any complex, highly sophisticated culture.

Consider the following: if in order for a phenomenon to occur only one "necessary condition" is required, the phenomenon has a relatively high probability of occurring. The greater the number of conditions that must occur simultaneously, however, the lower becomes the likelihood of occurrence; too many things have to happen or exist at the same time. It is entirely possible that the conditions favoring Keftian social stability were sufficiently numerous that they did occur simultaneously only once during the period in history when humans were moving from small communities to state level.

Women, Power, and the Biology of Peace

1. Protection from aggressors. The Keftians lived on an island sufficiently far from the mainland that they would have been protected from invasion and conquest while they passed, over hundreds of years, from tribal to community to state level. Clearly, without the protection of such isolation, any strong and unswerving inclination they had for peace would have doomed the culture in short order, as soon as they came under attack by aggressive neighbors.

2. Resources that enable self-sufficiency. Their island was a large one, able to provide all, or nearly all, critical resources to make the transition to state level. The Keftians could persist and "do their own thing" without being brought to their knees by outsiders upon whom they were critically dependent.

3. A legitimate, strong, central authority. Clearly Knossos was the center of the Keftian culture, the strong central authority that is one of the hallmarks of a state-level society. The reasons why Knossos rose to this status are not known, and may never be known.

Crete was poor in the metals (tin and copper) needed to make Bronze. At some point the Keftians must have made strategic alliances or trading contacts off-island because without such trading partners, they would have lacked these materials. One might suppose that the city/community (Knossos?) best able to make and keep such contacts might eventually have come to be the center of decision-making and distribution of these critical materials. Or perhaps the negotiating skills of members of the religious community at Knossos were superior, and as religion became centered there, so did other functions. It is entirely likely that a combination of events were responsible for elevating Knossos to central power and influence. Perhaps even the rise of a pivotal personality—perhaps a woman as High Priestess in Knossos who had the temperament and political skills of Elizabeth I, Queen of England (see below, p. 104).

4. An ethos of non-violence. Also necessary would have been a long-standing, shared religious or ethical tradition that was widespread on the island and that fostered a pacific lifestyle, perhaps similar to the Hopi culture of North America described by Frank Waters. An aversion to violence would have to have been deeply rooted in the culture to guide them through the stressful passage from local tribes, to larger communities, to state. Short of force, I can think of no influence sufficiently powerful to provide that kind of control and cohesion but religion.

A fifth condition seems to be strongly suggested by the rest of human history as also probably necessary:

5. Strong female influence. The female inclination for social stability would have been exercised through religion. The Keftians clearly maintained a tradition of goddess worship, so it is not improbable that women in their religion were not merely figureheads. If so, the female tendency to anticipate and resolve problems before they produce serious unrest could have found powerful expression. These people could have used the persuasive, even coercive, power of religion to foster peace and stability whenever more aggressive inclinations from any sources threatened to take the path to armed conflict.

6. Population Density Did Not Exceed Resource Availability. Finally, the Keftians must have made the transition to state level well before Crete's population density exceeded the island's capacity to provide any critical resource. Indeed, they must still have been quite resource rich.

One function of central authority is to control, regulate, and distribute vital resources, perhaps especially in times of stress due to crop failure or other natural disasters. If done to encourage social stability over the long haul, extreme disparities that lead to social unrest would not have developed.

When any critical resource—water, food, fuel, or land—is insufficient to supply the basic needs of all, the inevitable result is either emigration or physical conflict over that resource or both. This is true regardless of who runs the state—men, women, powerful families, or the people in a democracy. When physical conflict over resources becomes essential to survival, men will gain in power, and women will suffer a loss of it because women, being involved in child-bearing and rearing, will be at a disadvantage whenever society resorts to war in order to maintain resource control.

At least this was the situation during the Keftian period of history. To the extent that modern women now have the means to control their fertility and limit their offspring over their lifetimes; to the extent they live well and influentially into old age; and to the extent that the weapons of war do not require the body strength of a male to wage and win a conflict, women are in a position to participate more fully in modern power games over resources.

Ages waxed and waned. Keftian society passed from history, and knowledge of their special world died until rediscovery in 1 900CE. We will not likely ever know the reasons for their eclipse.

Yet we should not underestimate the significance of their accomplishment. Given what was necessary in order for the Keftian culture to develop and persist as long as it did, undisturbed and unconquered, while all cultures on the mainland were being swept, pushed, and pulled by war, it's not difficult to understand why they might be a lone example of what might have been. We can appreciate also how they can be a provocative model for what might one day be again.

Section III
Regulating Social Behavior

And what is one to do with treadmills for grinding corn, whose motive power is said by some to be the donkey, and by some the carrot in front of his nose?
    ❧ Stuart Chase, Economist

There is a homely adage which runs 'Speak softly and carry a big stick; you will go far.'
    ❧ Theodore Roosevelt

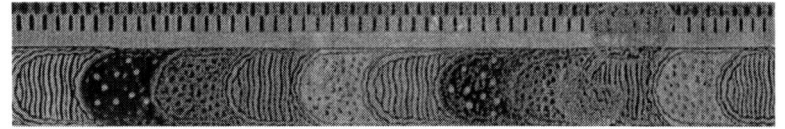

Regulating Social Behavior

*H*ow could a society that proposed to resolve its conflicts without violence deal with human misconduct? The Keftians, for example, surely experienced the usual rivalries and disagreements all humans living in large, complex, and socially stratified groups encounter. They were humans living in the real world, not saints or flower children living in a utopia. How might they have regulated their social behavior?

Shunning

In my novel I made the reasonable assumption that the Keftians had available for their use the same mechanisms of social control available to all societies—"carrot" and "stick." Reward and punishment.

Since their art depicts no images of any of the common forms of violent physical punishment, such as whipping or stoning or maiming, I envisioned that because of a peaceful ethos, they avoided those controls that employed extremes of aggression and force. That left them with the more subtle, negative persuasive tools of shunning (avoidance of contact) or ostracism (a stronger form of shunning where the offender is cast out from society, permanently or temporarily).

These negative social reinforcers—the "stick"—powerfully shape behavior because they are so unpleasant or even devastating to us both socially and emotionally. We're social primates to the core. We need to feel connected to the people around us who are our support group. For most people, being shunned by those close to us is nearly unbearable.

Shunning has been used to great effect by many religions to keep the behavior of their members in line: the American Mennonites, for example. Jehovah's Witnesses practice ostracism; if a member decides he or she can no longer accept the faith and rejects the group's standards, that person is socially cut off, even from their own families. Only if you are willing to abandon your family can you leave the religious fellowship, a profoundly painful choice; for many people a choice that is simply unthinkable.

A "time-out" imposed on a misbehaving child is really a mini-shunning. Boehm describes how the Utku of Alaska and other hunter-gatherers use ostracism to regulate social behavior. For most humans, being cut off from eye contact or speech for even a week is severe punishment.

If a culture is deeply steeped in a shared religion that embraces these behaviors and if that religion has the power to exert punishment for infractions, large or small, through techniques like shunning, even the largest, most complex society can enforce its shared values by non-violent means. All members of the group are collaborators that participate in the application of reinforcing, punishing behavior.

The ultimate shunning would be permanent expulsion from one's home and community and excommunication from one's religious body, leaving the offender thoroughly cut off from fellowship with the rest of society and from contact with the divine. To anyone who has suffered from the harsher applications of this form of social control, a secular system of laws, fairly applied and allowing freedom of action that doesn't harm others, is far more likely to be preferred to the strictures and conformity required to regulate behavior with shunning. While it does the job, shunning may leave little room for dissent, individuality, or creativity.

A Sacred Sex Hypothesis

As a compliment to the negative reinforcement of shunning, perhaps a powerfully positive force may have helped to regulate and pacify Keftian social behavior in a way to decrease violence—a carrot. I was prodded in this direction because speculation was useful as I tried to create a convincing but alien, women-centered, non-aggressive culture for the novel. I let my imagination run free.

Certainly when considering the roots of war and how war might be avoided, we do need to ask what factors could have caused or allowed the Keftians to be so extraordinarily different—not just uncommon but unique. Perhaps something quite unusual, quite unlike the many patriarchies that have shaped written history.

I suggest that their religion included sex as a religious and socially beneficial action that ritualized peace or harmony between the sexes. That sexual intercourse decreases aggression is well known; athletic coaches often discourage sex before a big game, as do generals preparing men for battle. **Such a religion may well have produced a people whose males were not obsessed or occupied primarily with war.**

I was led to this hypothesis initially because of the dress of the "snake goddesses" (see below) and because I knew that in many places in the ancient world, a form of "sacred" or religiously-associated prostitution was a respected profession. Ultimately, though, four lines of evidence became the sources of this "sacred sex" hypothesis for Keftian social control:

Evidence from Biology — Chimpanzees and Bonobos

When bonobos were first brought to the attention of western scientists, they were thought to be a subspecies of chimpanzee. They do strongly resemble chimps physically, at least to the untrained eye, but bonobos and chimpanzees are, in fact, two different species of ape. Chimpanzees can be found in a variety of forest habitats in Africa. Bonobos live in a rather restricted forest area in a part of Africa formerly known as the Congo. The ranges of the two apes don't overlap.

The DNA of both species has been compared to ours. Rather surprisingly, they both are more closely related to humans than they are to gorillas. So closely related to us genetically that Jared Diamond, in *The Third Chimpanzee,* proposes we could all be in the same scientific genus: *Homo sapiens (us), Homo troglodytes* (chimps), and *Homopaniscus* (bonobos).

In the wild, chimpanzees, like patriarchal cultures, have a social structure based on a hierarchy of dominance, with males at the top. They settle their disputes and social disagreements with aggressive-laden displays of dominance and submission. What's more, chimpanzees practice murder and infanticide and a kind of primitive war in which a group of chimps band together, invade a neighboring territory, and find and kill a member of the neighboring group.

Bonobos, on the other hand, live in the wild in a social world where the females are the focal members of the troops. Female bonobos have high status, with the dominant female and dominant male being co-equal. The male dominance hierarchy roughly parallels that of the females.

Whenever tensions erupt, bonobos often find resolution when members of the group engage in sex. All kinds of sex. Male/female, male/male, female/female, young/old. Even, most astonishingly when first observed, frontal sex, unknown among chimps.

When different bonobo groups meet at territory boundaries, agitation can occur and clashes can erupt. Occasionally these lead to bloody wounds. Bonobo groups are not without conflict, and the males are not without aggressive tendencies: for example, they form hierarchies. As, for that matter, do the females. Bonobos, too, are not flower children. But so far among them there are no recorded instances of either murder or infanticide or primitive warfare.

In one experiment, Takayoshi Kano had set out sugarcane as bait to attract bonobos so he could observe them, and he inadvertently placed the bait on the border of the ranges of two foraging groups. By chance the two groups arrived simultaneously. Tensions flared. While the males on both sides avoided each other, females from the two groups engaged in sex with each other and sometimes with males from the other group. **Bonobos use sex as both a bonding mechanism and a mechanism for diffusing social tension.**

Both apes are equally closely related to us genetically. What this suggests is that humans, who are astonishingly flexible when it comes to social and sexual behavior, may well in theory have the genetic capacity to organize themselves in a more bonobo-like than chimp-like fashion.

In fact, we share three traits with bonobos that appear to relate to female empowerment in ways that would imply that human social organization shares more with bonobos than with chimpanzees, or at least did so in our deep past. Richard Wrangham and Dale Peterson wrote a long exploration of the origins of aggressive human behavior called *Demonic Males: Apes and the Origins of Human Violence*. In two chapters, they compare human anatomy and behavior with the anatomy and behavior of chimpanzees and bonobos.

They present an interesting evolutionary scenario that might explain why chimps are so demonic and bonobos so peaceable. The essence is that female bonobos are able to restrain male bonobo aggression because bonobos eat foods that allow them to travel in slightly larger groups than chimps can. As a result, female bonobos have enough time together to form critical alliances that allow them to act together to prevent male domination.

By contrast, because of the foods chimps eat, they are forced to split into smaller groups. Unable to spend much time together, the female chimps aren't able to form strong female alliances. Consequently, in the wild, female chimps are not able to check male aggression.

Based on the abundant historical evidence of human wars and other expressions of human male dominance and aggression, Wrangham and Peterson conclude that when students of human evolution consider our deep past, they should use a chimpanzee model as a starting point for the study of human evolution. Christopher Boehm also accepts the chimpanzee model. He says he did so for the pragmatic reason that science knows more about chimpanzees and because he was also personally familiar with them. He also notes that chimpanzees are tool-using generalists that appear in a wide-variety of habitats, as do humans, while bonobos are not.

By accepting this assumption, however, an investigator is primed to accept that extreme male dominance and male aggression are the fundamental characteristics of human evolutionary ancestors and that females have been kept in their place from the time of our deep past.

I am more impressed that we share the following biological characteristics with bonobos:

- hidden ovulation
- positioning of the vagina and clitoris in a more ventral and forward position so that frontal sex is both possible and pleasurable (reinforcing)
- continuous female receptivity.

Recall that hidden ovulation makes it impossible for males to know when a female is fertile. Hidden ovulation makes it totally impractical for males to try to keep other males away from a female during her most fertile period since males cannot know the appropriate time to do female guarding. Since guarding is rendered essentially useless, male bonobos don't do it. This gives females greater flexibility and freedom to mate with males of their choice. Wrangham and Peterson recognize this and even point out how it empowers female bonobos. They seem to forget its significance, though, when they argue that early hominids were probably chimp-like, not bonobo-like.

It's also reasonable to assume that face-to-face sharing of pleasure serves to facilitate personal bonding. (Wrangham and Peterson vividly describe how this works to facilitate bonding between female bonobos.) The shifting of the female sexual structures to a more ventral/forward position in humans and bonobos very likely facilitates the use of sex by both species as a bonding mechanism rather than simply a mechanism for fertilization.

Further, it has been theorized that continuous female receptivity facilitates a female's ability to make bonds with one or more males that can serve her interests beyond fertilization, perhaps giving her protection or sharing food with her (such as animal kills) during other, non-fertile parts of her cycle.

To the extent that these exceptional shared physical traits suggest a more egalitarian social world between the sexes, students of human evolution need to shift their view of our deep past to allow for a more bonobo-like model of our hominid ancestors. At least certainly not a full-blown chimp one. A chimp model most probably is *not* an appropriate starting place. The chimps may just have proceeded ever further down their path to the demonic aggression described by Wrangham and Peterson while the bonobos proceeded down the path to the peaceableness we see now.

The truth for human ancestors probably lies somewhere in between the chimp and bonobo models, with the human specialization being flexibility. The social structure that developed for any given hominid group may have depended heavily on the availability and nature of local resources.

A more bonobo-like model for early human groupings would certainly fit better with Christopher Boehm's many examples of egalitarian behavior among hunter-gatherers where males and females are co-dominant and where both sexes often take lovers. (This taking of lovers is, by the way, the major cause of disharmony and even murder within these egalitarian communities.) It's likely, as I'll return to below, that humans didn't begin to shift strongly in the direction of chimpanzee social structure and behavior, with its strong male dominance, aggression, warfare, and extreme female subordination, until the agricultural revolution.

Evidence from Anthropology — The Canela of South America

A human society provides a second line of evidence for the sacred sex hypothesis, proof that at least in tribal groups of up to a thousand individuals, humans can use sex to facilitate social bonding and decrease social tensions. *The Canela: Social Bonding through Ritual, Kinship, and Sex,* by William and Jean Crocker, is a fascinating study of the Canela of South America.

The traditional lifestyle of these people was practiced until very recently when the outside world began to intrude. It's worth noting, because later I'll discuss the importance of young males to social stability, that young males were the first to begin chaffing under traditional customs.

Sex between men and women was frequent, including sex between couples not married to each other. The Canela recognized that these sexual liaisons served to foster social cohesion. The sharing of sex, for example, brought the sense that a child had many fathers, and this provided an extended sense of bonding within the community. Any man that had had sex with the woman, not just her husband, was the father of her child. These people were and still are very non-aggressive with each other in their daily lives.

What the Crockers describe is not free love. There were rules. Rules about when, where, and between whom sex was appropriate. Young people were taught the rules by their elders and were expected to conform to them. If they did not, their close relatives would correct them. If the infraction was serious, the community leader might be called in to set an individual straight.

For example, young men were not to have sex with a young girl before she was married. Indeed, young men were encouraged to have sex with older women, even post-menopausal women, as a means of preventing pregnancy of unmarried young girls. This was one of the rules with which young men first began to disagree. Sharing their wives with other men was another. Clearly, without strong rules and traditions, the power of sex to disrupt and create conflicts would soon defeat any potential bonding and pacifying benefits.

Evidence From the Keftians — The Keftian Snake Goddesses

One of the most identifiable symbols in Keftian art is the distinctive narrow-waisted, breast-exposing **Keftian dress** depicted in their frescoes, on vases, on seal stones, and in these famous figurines, called the Snake Goddesses (page 87).

Along with pubic hair, human female breasts are a "secondary sexual characteristic." Their blossoming indicates that a girl has become, or is becoming, a woman, capable of breeding. Enlarged breasts aren't needed for milk production—the females of other higher primates don't have enlarged breasts and they provide milk quite well for their young. But enlarged breasts, when still round and high in youth, attract human males and are highly sexual.

It's true that in cultures where women typically don't cover their breasts, men may not report breasts as being especially stimulating. And indeed, the breasts of women after they have children and nurse them aren't likely to be so. But young, full breasts are a cue, even if only a subconscious one, that a girl is ready to breed.

These unnaturally narrow-waisted Keftian figures with full and uplifted breasts reminded me of what biologists call a supernormal stimulus. A classic example of a super-normal stimulus comes from the study of gulls and their eggs. An investigator removed a gull from its nest, and out of sight of the bird, put two nests on the same spot, one nest holding the bird's own eggs and one with clearly much larger but otherwise similar looking eggs. When the released bird returned, it faced a choice: incubate its own eggs or the bigger ones. The gulls invariably chose the bigger eggs.

The stimulus of enhanced size is the attractor—it's a "supernormal" (exaggerated) stimulus, a highly attractive signal. Perhaps this remarkable Keftian dress served as an exaggerated signal or icon—in this case, a signal of sexuality associated with Keftian culture.

Some have suggested in response to my hypothesis that this unique Keftian dress was simply a matter of fashion and had no symbolism. Frescos that display these dresses, they say, may simply represent the gowns of fashionable ladies in a secular society.

While this is possible, it seems extremely unlikely. In the Bronze Age Keftian world of 1600 BCE, it is far more likely that religion and life were inseparable, and that virtually all events represented in their art had religious or social/historical significance. Rather than the frescos depicting ladies of fashion, it seems more likely that the dress may have been associated with religion and that the figures wearing it likely were priestesses or worshippers. In contexts that don't seem particularly religious, such as the scene in Akrotiri Town, other dresses are represented.

When I first discovered the Keftians, I wanted to like them because they so obviously respected women. The snake goddesses' tiny waists and exposed breasts, though, disturbed me. I was young and sexually naive. To make my peace with them, I decided that they must represent nurturing—the maternal essence of a mother goddess. I am now at the other end of my life, and it is quite clear that these are sensual figures. They are not motherly. They are not nurturing. In any culture they exude messages of both power and sex.

Figure 10: Snake Goddesses

Evidence From The Tradition of Sacred Prostitution

A tradition in classical Greece provided a final hint about what Keftians may have been doing. Religious traditions are extremely resistant to change or deletion. They often persist in some form, perhaps highly modified, long after the time when their original meaning or function was understood. In some cities in classical Greece, temple prostitution was a respected custom.

Corinth, for example, was famous for its temple to Aphrodite. Men could go to one of these women dedicated to Aphrodite and experience the gift of the goddess in the arms of one of her servants.

I select this example of mixing sex and the sacred from the geographic region of the Mediterranean because it represents something that, however altered, might possibly be linked back in time to the Keftians. But certainly many traditions from cultures far from Crete mingle sex and the sacred. Perhaps the best-known current example would be forms of tantric Hinduism.

The implications of such a custom for modern societies that are products of millennia of various forms of patriarchy are potentially staggering. Imagine the world today if people could go to a church, a temple, or a mosque for expert, experienced, safe sex and know that the act was acceptable, even blessed. What would be the consequences of a religious affirmation that all coupling, not just that of marriage, is a celebration of life? A celebration of the gift of physical pleasure? A celebration of harmonious connectedness between men and women, male and female?

I'm often asked if women in the classical Greek period enjoyed the same freedom to go to a temple for sex? No. But the Greeks lived hundreds of years after the Keftians. By classical Greek times, the Keftian independence of women that might have made such sexual equality possible had been, in my view, vastly reduced.

Is it possible that the Keftians were far more bonobo- than chimplike? There is that old saying, "Make love, not war." The Keftians may have been doing exactly that.

The Ideal of Romantic Love

Immediately we are set to wondering what effect such inclusive sexual relations—the practice of sexual activity with persons other than one's spouse—might have on marriage. Most particularly, what effect would it have on the decidedly Western concept of marriage based on romantic love between husband and wife "till death do us part?"

Recall first that throughout history, the more common practice has been to arrange marriages for reasons having nothing to do with "love." In many cultures, this is still the case. An attraction between the pair might have been considered, but often the choices were based on financial or other resource considerations, on what assets one or the other of the couple might bring to the marriage and the raising of children. The man and woman were neither required nor necessarily expected to grow to "love" each other.

We might reexamine the Canela data and ask whether there were married couples in the community who, in spite of having sex with other individuals, nevertheless formed attachments to each other that we associate with committed love. Sociologists who study so-called "swingers," couples who are married to each other but regularly engage in sex with other individuals, can also make a contribution to the question. Doubtless it will be true in every case, as it was true for the Canela, that having clear rules for what is acceptable and what is not would be essential to avoid creating more conflict than harmony.

Giving the blessings of society to consensual sex would change many of the assumptions we have taken for granted, at first with most unsettling results. There would surely be a period of serious turmoil as new rules were established. It is possible, in fact, to argue that such changes are already happening in many Western societies, with men and women being unsure exactly what the new "dating rules" and "marriage rules" are.

But this doesn't mean the ideal of romantic love would die. Nor would we necessarily abandon the responsibilities and joys of sharing in raising children conceived out of love. It would appear to be too satisfying, too life-enhancing, to those who live in such voluntary commitment for free men and women to give it up as the ideal. Indeed, at least in Western societies, those who are happiest, male and female, have been shown by many studies to be those who live their lives in a long-term, committed bond of love. Other arrangements may "work," but they don't generally provide the same degree of personal satisfaction or produce the same degree of personal growth.

Section IV
Women and Warfare

Battle life has swallowed me completely. I can't seem to think of anything but the fighting. I'm burning to chase the Germans from our country so we can lead a normal happy life together again.
> ❧ Lily Litvak - Russian flying ace, WW II
> ❧ Quoted in Kate Muir's *Arms and the Woman*

Women and Warfare

*I*n my view, since the agricultural revolution, since we left the hunter/gatherer way of life behind, we have slowly but steadily shackled Venus, and Mars has been running rampant. And it hasn't been a pretty picture.

Agricultural Revolution and the Shift in Balance of Power between the Sexes

What has brought us to our current state of affairs?

Resources influence power relations between people and nations in critical ways, a subject fully explored by Jared Diamond in his masterful book, *Guns, Germs, and Steel*. When referring to the onset of massive changes in the history of human societies, he says, "It was only within the last 11,000 years that some peoples turned to what is called food production: that is, domesticating wild animals and plants and eating the resulting livestock and crops." From this pivotal change, he explores the unfolding of subsequent history of war and conquest between cultures and nations.

Resources also influence power relations between the sexes. And I, too, pick agricultural revolution as a pivotal turning point. Agricultural revolution is a time when the control of vital food resources begins to shift. Food goes from being something that is simply gathered (or hunted) and brought back home for, most commonly, immediate consumption, to a major resource that can be stored and controlled by a few determined and armed individuals. Whenever humans grow ever more dependent on hoardable and defendable resources, those who are willing and able to use threats or violence to do the hoarding (or stealing) gain power over those who are dependent on the resource.

In most hunter-gatherer societies, women wield impressive influence. They bring in and control vital food supplies for their family. They may even gather sufficient material to share within the group at large, but families are, generally speaking, independent food-consuming units.

Marjorie Shostak provides an example in *Nisa. The life and words of a !Kung woman.* The !Kung of the African Kalahari desert are the people of the diminutive hero of the movie, *The Gods Must Be Crazy.* !Kung men and women have essentially equal status, and the women, who are gatherers of mostly plant materials, are recognized as being the group's primary economic providers. As in many societies where the men are hunters and occasionally bring in the prized delicacy of protein-rich meat, there is a special appreciation for this hunting skill. But Boehm makes very clear the many ways the !Kung make sure no "upstart" hunter male is able to use this ability to gain higher status than any other member of the group.

Because women are generally deeply involved in the demanding process of child-bearing and rearing, they are disadvantaged when it comes to devoting great amounts of time to weaponry and fighting. When groups grow to sufficient size that they have become dependent upon hoardable resources that can be controlled by threat or force or aggression (typically these are produced by the tools of agriculture), women inevitably lose power—seriously so.

Women As Warriors

This is not to say that women cannot or will not fight—history makes clear they will. There is no doubt among people who love their freedom that some wars had to be fought. For Americans and many others, the Second World War is a prime example. Women are just as aware of this reality as men and as mindful of the necessity, sometimes, to fight and win.

A recent mini-flood of books has explored the subject of women who were warriors. In *Arms and the Woman,* for example, Kate Muir focuses principally on modern combat, from such battles as the Gulf War of 1991 to the WW II Special Operations Executive (SOE) organized by the British as resistance fighters and behind-the-lines saboteurs in France.

She thoroughly describes the success of women in the Gulf war. They served on ships. They served as pilots and as ground troop support. "They loaded the ammunitions and set the computer co-ordinates for the Patriot anti-missile batteries that took on Saddam Hussein's Scuds."

Muir also gives realistic assessments of the significant difficulties the women encountered while serving, from dealing with resentful males to having menstrual periods under trying circumstances to getting pregnant. She also describes the significant difficulties the services had in trying to integrate women into what had been an all-male world.

Her conclusion: under the conditions of modern warfare, there is no reason to exclude women as a group from any tasks. And I would argue that if women's influence is to be felt in the military, something that would be critical to the ultimate goal of achieving social balance and stability, they must serve or have no credibility in debate and no grounds to speak with authority in matters military.

Only in the infantry, says Muir, where size and strength are all-important, are women unlikely to ever be qualified in great numbers. But, she argues, the few women who can meet identical stringent physical requirements for men and want to serve on the front lines should be allowed to.

Muir also describes the British Special Operations Executive (SOE) that worked with the resistance in France to sabotage the occupying Germans. This was a high-risk enterprise. Volunteers were sent behind the lines into unfamiliar territory. They had to find a resistance group and then organize communications and guerilla actions. Because they were less likely to raise suspicion, women were ideal secret agents; of 469 people who served in the SOE, 39 were women.

The main qualification for acceptance in the SOE was the ability to speak fluent French, and a number of "seemingly very ordinary" women signed on. Muir recounts the story of one of these, Odette Churchill. Caught by the Germans, she was imprisoned in Paris and tortured. They put a red-hot poker on her back. They tore out her toenails. She was imprisoned for over a year at the women's concentration camp at Ravensbrük. Unlike another SOE woman, Violet Szabo who was executed there, Churchill survived. When she returned to England she was awarded the George Cross. These were women who not only fought, they fought well and with courage.

Muir also describes, as does Jessica Amanda Salmonson in the *Encyclopedia of Amazons,* women warriors of the past. We learn of the record of Hippocrates in the fifth century BCE concerning the Sauromatian women who "ride, shoot, and throw javelins while mounted." And we learn about archeological discoveries from this same region dating to the third and fourth century BCE where women are buried with what are clearly a warrior's belongings.

Traditionally this region north of the Black Sea, in the Ukraine and Southern Russia, has been associated with the Amazons of Greek fame, and these burials have revitalized the idea that Amazons were something more than mythological creatures. Jeannine Davis-Kimball has published studies undertaken in this region and also has a book, *Warrior Women: An Archaeologist's Search for History's Hidden Heroines*. Muir, citing Davis-Kimball's work, tells us about the burial of one of these women. Those who laid her to rest gave her such feminine objects as bronze and silver bracelets, a necklace of glass beds, a bronze mirror, and a Greek amphora, but in addition, by her head lay two iron lance blades and she had a quiver of twenty arrows and a woman-sized suit of iron-scale armor.

Salmon son's book, *The Encyclopedia of Amazons*, lists female warriors from the present going back into the ancient past. For each entry, an information snippet tells a bit about the woman and usually explains the context in which she fought.

Salmonson defines an Amazon as a woman who is a "duelist or soldier, by design or circumstances, whether chivalrous or cruel, and who engages others in direct combat, preferably with some semblance of skill and honorability." "Spies, assassins, modern frontline technicians, famous criminals, modern athletes, explorers, orators, big-game hunters and mothers saving their children from wild beasts were not included." Still, the remaining list is impressively long.

Defense vs. Offense

One comes away from these books, and others like them, knowing that women have fought bravely and successfully throughout history. What is less clear, or at least not explicitly explored, is whether these women warriors fought in what they perceived to be wars of aggression or wars of defense, or simply fought because they had no choice or because they enjoyed it. Were they the instigators and leaders of these enterprises, or merely swept up into the conflict?

In the Kingdom of Dahomey in West Africa during the 1800s there supposedly lived genuine Amazons. The impression I always was given as I read about them was that these were fierce women, in charge of their own lives, who had chosen a life of war. Muir looks a bit deeper.

She explains that the Dahomey were "ruled by a ruthless king, usually portrayed as fond of displaying piles of his enemies' severed heads." He was indeed surrounded by a bodyguard of fierce women warriors, at its height a group of around 4,000 women. They had status equal to the male warriors. According to Salmonson, some had multiple husbands. They apparently often went bare-chested and would train by leaping over burning barriers and running barefoot through thorn thickets.

Muir notes that these women were recruited every three years when the king's subjects had to bring their teenage daughters to the king for selection. She states that the strongest and most intelligent girls were chosen as officers, and the rest were either rejected or became foot soldiers. This was clearly conscription, not voluntary service. And the organizer and instigator was a king, not a queen.

Muir also tells the compelling tale of Lily Litvak, a Russian ace pilot. In the Second World War, the Russians were so desperate for troops that they took some 800,000 women into the military. These women learned to be snipers, fighter pilots, drivers in tank battalions, submachine gunners in the infantry, and medical orderlies. In 1942, Lily Litvak joined the 73rd Fighter Regiment.

She was just five feet tall, slight, with blonde hair and the reflexes and instincts of a great fighter pilot. After several spectacular kills, Muir says she gained such a reputation that German pilots could be heard yelling on their radios, "**Achtung,** Litvak!" Her nickname was "The White Rose of Stalingrad," and a white rose was painted on her plane.

She brought down ten German aircraft. A day before she died in an air battle she wrote home, "Battle life has swallowed me completely. I can't seem to think of anything but the fighting. I'm burning to chase the Germans from our country so we can lead a normal happy life together again." Great courage, lots of fighting spirit, and marshaled in the cause of defense!

Women, Power, and the Biology of Peace

Female mammals, including female primates, are typically, within their physical and behavioral limits, fierce fighters in defense of their young. With humans it seems quite likely this strong inclination to defend one's young could be extended to include defense of the community where one is raising those young. Or even to the defense of one's society or culture if the prospect of that society's or culture's falling creates underlying fear that the security in which one will raise one's young is threatened.

History certainly shows that women sufficiently roused to take up arms can be determined and in some cases brutal, vicious, and vengeful fighters. But what moves them to these actions? How often are women not defenders but active instigators in wars of aggression or expansion? How often do women seek to use aggression to take the territory of others?

One objection often raised to me when I suggest that women are less likely to be roused to war is, "What about Margaret Thatcher?" But England's Maggie Thatcher did not invade Argentina. Argentina had invaded the Falklands, an island with people of British origins and culture who begged assistance from the homeland. Golda Meir, the Israeli Prime Minister associated with the 1973 October War in Palestine, also comes readily to mind as a woman who led her people in time of war. But once again, she acted in response to being attacked.

Are women aggressors or defenders? Salmonson's encyclopedia allows us to make a rough assessment of this question using a fairly good-sized sample. Her A–Z listing is impressive, with the qualification that inclusion of a great many goddesses and mythical women gives it a weight not entirely based in reality.

I noted the reason Salmonson gives as the motivating factors or contexts in which these women fought, using women in the A–B and the T–Z sections of the alphabet, a choice that gave me a randomly selected list of 336 total names. After I eliminated the goddesses and mythical women and women for whom not enough information was given to put their fighting into a context, a sample of 110 remained.

Salmonson says, "I have given special consideration to active defenders of castles." She says she does this because some critics argue that castle defense isn't sufficiently active and so shouldn't count as making a woman a warrior. They argue that such a woman is simply waiting for besiegers to tire and go home.

She replies that defense against siege *is* active participation, and so she includes such women, so long as they took up arms and directed operations. (I'm glad she did or the results would be skewed heavily toward other reasons for taking up arms. It would also have made her list of female warriors much shorter.) She argues: "It is, in fact, nobler and no less dangerous than offense even if I must confess that I find the *several instances* of women setting out to take castles especially thrilling moments in history." (Emphasis mine)

Only several instances? This was my first hint that I might not find many examples of female acts of conquest.

She includes heroines of a "chivalrous or warlike nature." Those of chivalrous nature I assume are perhaps freedom fighters or defenders of one sort or another. I don't question that women born into high status in a warrior culture may take up arms to defend the right of their young, their lineage, to inherit this same high status. Defense of one's high rank by female primates by fighting (or not uncommonly for humans, by poisoning one's rivals) is well known. But it is those women of true "warlike nature" who would be most relevant here: women in the grip of a lust for power. Lust for territory. The generators of war. Women who, in order to *achieve* high status or to make their status rise to even greater heights, started wars of conquest or continued a husband's campaigns.

Table 1 presents the results. If the "chivalrous" categories of Defense of Castle, Country, or Throne, Overthrow of Oppressive Regime, and Resisting Captors/Avenging a Loved One/Or To Be

Motivation	Number	Examples
Defense of castle, country, or throne	58	Agrippina the Younger Tamara of Georgia
Overthrow oppressive regime/rebellion	19	Boadicea Harriet Tubman
Fighting against captors, personal revenge, or to be with a lover or husband	8	Sofie Vansa Princess Wolonsky
Pirates/Raiders	6	Anne Bonney Nancy Walker
Adventurer	6	Eliza Allen Loreta Velasquez
Conquest	1	Agrippina the Elder enobia
Because of religious visions	1	Caterina Benincasa

Table 1: Reasons Women Took Up Arms

With a Lover are combined, they total 85 cases or 77.3% of the reasons why women took up arms. This quick sampling is tantalizing evidence that defense of one sort or another is the chief reason women take up arms.

Pirates and Raiders seems to be a category of women on their society's fringes who found status and made a living by questionable means in terms of honor, but they did not instigate war. They are roughly 5.5% of the sample.

The same is true for the Adventurers, another 5.5%. These were virtually all women who lusted for something other than the humdrum and enlisted in wars started by others. It would be interesting to know why they picked a particular side. Was the nature of the cause at all relevant to their choices?

Those women involved in wars of conquest (12) are 10.9% of the cases, even though a number of them simply accompanied their husbands into battles being waged in a foreign territory. The women themselves were often not the instigators of the original conflict, but because they actively took up arms and went to a foreign field, I included them. This makes the percentage in the female Conquerors category actually higher than the reality.

To measure the extent to which men and women differ in taking up arms, we would need to do a similar examination of the motives of equally prominent warriors in history. Curiously, I found no lists of males equivalent to Salmonson's volume, no books with a title like *Famous Warriors in History*. There are books on famous battles, and biographies of famous warriors, but I found no handy listing of history's most famous male warriors giving the reason they took up arms.

So we turn to *The 100: A Ranking of the Most Influential Persons in History,* by Michael Hart. It, too, gives thumbnail sketches of a number of people, in this case not selected as warriors but as individuals the author considers as having had the greatest impact on history. He listed them in his estimated order of most significant to least significant. The book makes fascinating reading in part because of his ranking.

The list includes some remarkably obscure names, for example ranked at #7 is Ts'ai Lun, the man who invented paper. There are 98 men in the top 100—two women made the list: Isabella I and Elizabeth I. It is encouraging that most of the men are great men of ideas (Newton, Einstein, Darwin, Copernicus, Edison, Plato, etc.), or religious thinkers (Mohammad, Jesus, Buddha, Confucius, Lao Tzu, Mahavira), or artists (Beethoven, Michelangelo, Bach, Picasso), and others whose contributions did not include war.

When their short biographies are examined, a rather ugly picture emerges in which men and one woman who were not themselves warriors, chivalrous or otherwise, created or promoted ideas that brought war or suffering as enormous as any war: Stalin, Hitler, Machiavelli, Umar ibn al-Khattab (leader of the most important Arab conquests), and Isabella I (the Inquisition).

Nevertheless, Hart chose 21 men who at some point took up arms.

- Five (23.81%) were Revolutionaries (Lenin, Mao Tse-tung, George Washington, Simon Bolivar, Oliver Cromwell).
- Sixteen (76.2%) were Conquerors who launched wars into territories not their own. Most are well known: Augustus Caesar, Genghis Khan, Alexander the Great, Napoleon Bonaparte, and so forth.

None of the men were Defenders. This is for the obvious reason that the list was drawn up not just to indicate that men could and would and had fought (abundantly self-evident for men), which was the point Salmonson was making with her list that included every notable woman who had ever taken up a weapon. Rather, the list was selected to represent people who made the greatest historical impact. Merely defending something (one's castle or even one's throne or country) is clearly less likely to have a major impact than launching a war.

Although we can't make a direct comparison from these very different lists, we can restrict the sample of women to revolutionaries versus conquerors, the same two categories we have for men. If we do, we see a revealing difference.

	Conquerors	Revolutionaries
Men	76.19%	23.81%
Women	38.7%	61.3%

Table 2 Conquerors vs. Revolutionaries

12 out of 31 such women (38.7%) were conquerors while 19 of the 31 (61.3%) were revolutionaries.

This compares to the 76.19 percent of the males who were conquerors and the 23.81 percent who were revolutionaries. The pattern is clearly reversed.

Salmonson and Hart set their own standards of selection for their lists and made the judgments about motivations or conditions affecting each listed individual. It's certain that some historians would disagree with some of their assessments. Still, the exercise throws light on two points.

First, the principle of the overlapping, albeit offset, bell curve holds even here in the matter of conquest. It's not that there are NO women motivated by conquest. Rather, that their numbers are small, both historically and as a percentage of notable women who have taken up arms for any reason.

Second, when we look at history, at who has made the greatest impact for good or ill, all of the conquerors who took up arms and made the top 100 are male.

So what of the famous Cleopatra (a woman in "C" of the alphabetical list, which was not in my sample)? Salmonson indicates that Cleopatra is a genuine example of female megalothymia (a lust for power—see **The Need for Recognition as an Engine of History** below). At least as described by Salmonson, Cleopatra appears to fit the profile of Conqueror, along with Catherine the Great and Semiramis (if she was real, not mythological). These are additional women of the female bell curve who, along with Agrippina the Elder and Xenobia, overlap the bell curve for men when it comes to conquest.

What of Elizabeth I, one of the two women who made Hart's 100? According to Salmonson, Elizabeth never led her troops in battle, and so she doesn't qualify to be a warrior. According to Hart, the great Elizabeth not only did not involve herself in campaigns of conquest, she did not involve her people either. Her diplomatic and political skills brought to England a long period of stability, a Golden Age, during which literature and exploration flourished. Elizabeth

I wisely built the island's navy into a formidable force, one that was able to repel the Spanish threat in the battle with the Spanish Armada. But she did not use this impressive military resource for offense. The expansion of England into empire came well after her enlightened reign. A comparison with another island world, the Crete of the Keftians, comes immediately to my mind.

It's important to remember to look beyond the specific individual. There are always individuals who don't fit the general pattern of their sex, but we are discussing the statistically significant differences in inclinations of males and females as groups. Any woman who could fight her way to the top and remain there in a patriarchal society and from that platform launch a war of aggression is going to have what we would call strongly masculine inclinations. She will also be an uncommon find.

Women, Cycles of Defense (Revenge), and Raiding for Resources

I discussed earlier six conditions I believe were necessary for the Keftians to achieve a highly complex, stratified culture through peaceful means. One was their isolation from aggressive neighbors. Another was an abundance of all (or nearly all) essential resources. It's not surprising, then, that most other chapters of human history, even among tribal, egalitarian societies, are marked by warfare. Rarely do people live in secure isolation from neighbors, and control of resources is a notable and obvious driving force behind wars. And we find two situations where women, even in egalitarian hunter-gatherer conditions, often support war—revenge cycles and raids for resources.

Note that the notion that simple (non-stratified, tribal) cultures did not practice war or had low death rates from wars (or raiding) is not supported by the evidence. Not all tribal cultures are warlike, but all are also not peaceful. It has been suggested that *per capita*, death rates in some tribal societies from between-group conflicts may actually exceed *per capita* death rates from wars in state-level societies.

One common pattern of behavior strongly resembles the earlier described primitive raids of chimpanzees. Warriors band together to attack a neighboring group. A well-known example is the patriarchal Yanomamö, studied in South America by Napoleon Chagnon.

Heated debate presently rages over Chagnon's work and over his conclusion that the principal resource gained by the warriors is access to women as mating partners. The women are either taken in the raids or are raped, or particularly fierce warriors (those known to have killed other men) were said to have more wives and more offspring than other men in their group. Controversy aside, there is little doubt that these tribal people, and many others like them, find themselves in vicious cycles of attack and counter-attack where revenge is an important motivating ingredient.

Tribal cultures aren't the only ones that can find themselves in a revenge quagmire. We're reminded of this almost daily when we contemplate the messes in Northern Ireland or Palestine, or even when we consider the legendary grudge between the American Hatfields and McCoys.

Once these violent patterns are set in motion, they are extraordinarily difficult to stop. This is principally because each side feels it is defending itself. Each side recites previous examples of violence by the other side as it prepares to launch its own retaliation. The logic is that if their side doesn't demonstrate its strength, the enemy will grow bolder, and their side will ultimately lose ground if not be entirely eliminated.

All too often neither side can bring off a definitive win, nor can they get enough psychological distance from the situation to find a way out. The cycle continues with both sides losing people and squandering resources, a situation experts in negotiation call lose-lose.

It's rather striking to note that cycles of attack and counter-attack occur even when the social milieu *within* a group maybe both egalitarian and nonviolent. Treatment of and behavior toward "others" is often quite different from and much more violent than the behavior practiced among "ourselves" (see below—**The Study of Existing Women-centered Cultures**). As we have seen, women can be fierce in matters of defense. Because of this, they are quite vulnerable to the appeal of defense against implacable, evil others and may even staunchly support a "preemptive" war.

On the other hand, if, as described by Fisher in *The First Sex*, women are more inclined to habitually think forward to anticipate problems (and surely this would include problems that might lead to future deadly conflicts), we should see a difference between egalitarian and patriarchal societies as women's priorities temper male ones. Unfortunately, no societies are ever identical except for the degree to which they are egalitarian or patriarchal. So it becomes difficult to make legitimate comparisons. In theory, if my hypothesis is true, all other factors being equal, egalitarian societies where women's voices have significant weight would find ways to terminate such feuds sooner than or would have fewer feuds than patriarchal societies.

A second case where women have frequently supported war occurs when raiding allows the warriors to bring back genuinely valuable resources. This sets up a dilemma for the women who must choose between the value of the resource that may be brought back and the costs the women may have to pay when their enemies in turn attack them. One can imagine superheated debates in egalitarian communities as the men and women struggle to determine where their true, long-term best interests lie. Again, if my hypothesis is correct and all other factors were equal, egalitarian groups would more frequently (but not necessarily always) reject the war option than would patriarchal groups.

Breaking Free

Peace won't just happen. The fundamental biological root of war (an aggressive male bonding tendency that can be controlled but not eliminated) and the practice of war itself extend deeply into our evolutionary past. If we want peace for our future's children, we'll need to exercise great ingenuity and determination to put the necessary conditions for peace into place. It may require that we take up the challenge to wage peace with the same passion and sacrifice that motivates us during war.

Certainly these two critical elements must be mastered: breaking and preventing revenge cycles and distributing the earth's resources equitably. And our most pressing need with respect to both problems is not for new information or further studies. We've had experts studying these issues for years.

The second half of William Ury's book, *Getting To Peace*, for example, lays out detailed steps to facilitate more win-win and less lose-lose conflict resolution. As for how the earth's resources can be best preserved and more equitably distributed, we've created mountains of books and scholarly papers with equally compelling insights and plans that can set us in the right direction. Douglas P. Fry, in *The Human Potential For Peace*, examines peaceful cultures and even ones without war and he describes the cultural mechanism they use to resolve conflicts nonviolently (see also the web site www.PeacefulSocieties.org).

No, our most pressing need is the will to act in accordance with what we claim to desire. Or perhaps it is the need to open our eyes and hearts to the vision of what changes are required. As citizens, we need to demand that our leaders set a high priority on proactively Waging Peace (not just reactively waging war against terrorists or terrorism). Then we need to watch whether they exercise power to *deliver* the conditions that foster peace. Then those of us in democratic societies need to vote with this end in mind.

Women, Power, and the Biology of Peace

The vote is not our only weapon in the battle for peace. There are others, like allocating personal and civic money appropriately, harnessing the dedication of armies of determined, peace-seeking individuals, and building a global community with an unswerving vision of a stable, peaceful world. But the vote is the most accessible tool and the touchstone for all the rest. Through the vote, we empower the will of all the people, not just the will of those especially aggressive individuals, male or female, who would dominate others.

This will surely be a messy process. Democracy is a messy process. But to quote Winston Churchill, "...it has been said that democracy is the worst form of Government, except all those other forms that have been tried from time to time."

Section V
Waging Peace

To jaw-jaw is better than to war-war.
      ✺ Winston Churchill

The ballot is stronger than the bullet.
      ✺ Abraham Lincoln

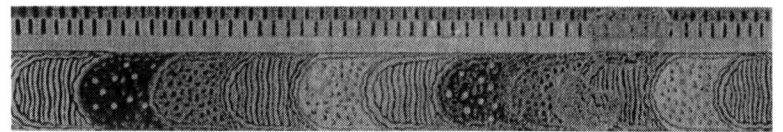

A Vision of a Peaceful Future and How to Get There

*M*y goal in Women, Power, and the Biology of Peace is to present ideas to provoke reflection and discussion. I don't believe that I, or for that matter anyone else, could sit down and in one book armchair a blueprint for the changes required to create a future without war. The task is staggeringly complex. Any attempt to predict outcomes of major social changes that will be needed is like attempting to predict the weather two years away, and about as useful.

To a great extent, we'll be working blindly. Our vision of what we will create will be less clear than we would like for the obvious reason that we cannot control everything that will happen. But assuming we make the choice to pursue the goal of a more stable world, many additional critical issues will have to be addressed, and in this section I highlight some of them. I'll also suggest preliminary steps we can take to hasten our advance.

Women, Power, and the Biology of Peace

Taming the Male Urge to Dominate

Hidden Females–To Solve a Problem We Need to Know What the Problem Is

When I first entered the field of animal behavior, specifically primatology virtually all major works on baboons had been written by men: Irven Devore, Sherwood Washburn, Irwin Bernstein, Stewart Altmann. Baboons are primates, savannah dwellers in many parts of Africa, related to us but not so closely as chimps or gorillas.

These researchers spent hundreds of hours observing their subjects, and the guiding theory the investigators developed to explain the working of the baboon world was that males were forever locked in competition with other males for dominance. The male biological goal was said to be to rise to the top of the hierarchy to become the dominant male, the big alpha who would mate with the most females when females came into breeding condition. Because of his dominance, a successful alpha male would leave more offspring.

Striving for dominance, it was said, was critical to reproductive success. "Baboons do this, baboons do that," these investigators would write. It was all about male striving and male dominance. I took it all in.

Then Jeanne Altmann, the wife of one of these investigators, entered the arena. She became curious about something quite different. What, she wondered, were the females up to? Were they only passive observers of all this male strutting and power grasping?

She found that females of the species she was studying, yellow baboons (*Papio cyanocephalus*), were not passive. Indeed, they had their own agendas. Her works, including *Baboon Mothers and Infants,* gave us remarkable new insights in several ways. Perhaps her chief contribution was to devise a new method of sampling.

In previous studies, the investigator usually sat down with a recording device or protocol sheet and observed what was happening in an *ad libitum* fashion. If an interaction caught the investigator's attention, he recorded it.

This led to obvious sampling biases because flashy interactions got the most attention. Jeanne Altmann decided to be more systematic and watch one individual for a given period of time, the "focal animal," and record everything that animal did, boring or not, and who it interacted with, even if all they did was sit together quietly grooming. After a fixed period of time, she shifted her attention to a different animal and gave it the same close attention. This included watching the females.

The results were as startling as if someone who is red-green color-blind had suddenly been given full color vision, particularly with respect to the females. A female baboon inherits her mother's dominance rank when she is quite young and she keeps this rank throughout her life. Consequently, an observer sees little overt aggression between females, but status is critically important to them. They defer to each other according to their rules of dominance, and they use behavior to reinforce their status, such as forcing a less dominant female to move from a choice resting place. These relatively quiet interactions reflect a long-established hierarchy so that a female baboon's social world, when it comes to rank, is quite stable for life.

Young males, on the other hand, are involved in a male world of continuous effort to rise in rank or to avoid losing status, just as other investigators had said. Agitation and aggressive interaction abound to catch an investigator's eye.

And what of the much-touted theory that the reason the males struggled to be at the top of the dominance hierarchy was to become the dominant male who mated with all females in heat? To be, in essence, the *only* breeding male in the group? Altmann was unable to prove paternity with the methods available to her at the time, but what she observed was fascinating.

Very high-ranking males often "herded" females. Herding is the same as guarding, described earlier. The male stays by a female and drives off any other male that might approach her. Females don't overtly fight against or protest such herding. On the other hand, females selectively avoid certain males when the male begins to approach, even high-ranking males. They can reciprocate the following of a particular male: the pair trade off following each other as they forage. Or then again, the females may not reciprocate the following of a male. And perhaps of most interest, they selectively follow and groom certain males, not all of whom are especially high ranking.

Female baboons are not passive at all. They're just not flashy. Subsequent work has shown that quite often when a dominant male is distracted and not paying close attention to a female in heat (the time during which these males take herding most seriously), a female may slip away. She may meet a male of her choice, one with whom she has spent time while not in heat. And she may mate with that male instead of the dominant one. These special male partners are never sub-adults, nor are they ones at the bottom of the male hierarchy. But they are not always the dominant male either.

Top, or alpha, males do perform a lot of mating. In general, females tend to favor strong males as a mating partner. By doing so, a female makes it more likely that her son will inherit genes for sufficient moxie to make his way to the top of the heap when he enters prime breeding age. So by choosing to mate with dominant, aggressive males, females actually play an important part in the evolution of male aggression as expressed in status-seeking.

The point here, however, is that after Altmann's work, one had to say, "Male baboons do this. Female baboons also do this, but they also do this other." Females were no longer hidden under the generalization "baboons." As long as females were considered just another baboon (and consequently ignored), the world of baboons could never be seen in its full reality.

Others interested in what females were doing followed Jeanne Altmann, such as Barbara Smuts who gave us *Sex and Friendship in*

Women, Power, and the Biology of Peace

Baboons. We learned that females make alliances with adult males who might not actually be the dominant male because these male "friends" buffer the female's offspring from other members of the group. They even serve as a buffer between the female herself and other male and female group members.

For example, baboon newborns are objects of intense curiosity. Females of low rank appear to suffer a great deal of stress when more dominant females approach and try to "pull" their baby away. But when the female and her offspring are with a male protector who is dominant over any female, the new mother can relax.

Having a male "friend" as a protector may well be a precursor for the male/female bond of marriage. Indeed, some have speculated that the purpose of "marriage" in pre-human ancestors may well have been not so much to protect females and their young from dangerous outsiders like lions or even to encourage a male to bring home meat, but to gain protection from troublesome individuals within the female's own group.

When I wrote my dissertation on Western Gulls, male investigators had also written the major gull papers: Nikko Tinbergen, John Coulson, Martin Moynihan. I assimilated their view that male gulls, being bigger, dominated the smaller females. I assumed this held true even among the males and females in the mated pairs I was studying. Mated females, for example, had been described as "begging" for food from their mates, both while they were forming the pair-bond and while the female was making eggs.

Then over a friendly cup of coffee at a scientific meeting a female biologist, Susan Smith, asked, "Are you quite certain the male partners you are observing dominate their mates? Are you sure the female's signal should properly be described as 'begging?'" I wasn't at all sure. And as I investigated further, I discovered to my quite honestly delighted surprise that within my bonded pairs, mated gulls behaved as equals.

As with baboons, an important reality of the life of gulls had been missed until the behavior of females was examined in more focused detail. Conflicts between Western Gull mates are resolved by egalitarian behavior rather than dominance and submission. For example, mates share food or practice a first-come-first-served rule over choice food tidbits. The signal that earlier had been called begging is more correctly described as soliciting or demanding—because if a male doesn't provide enough food to a hungry female who is making eggs, she may very well pick a different mate next year. Or refuse to bond with him this year.

The late Nobel Laureate Konrad Lorenz was a passionate and keen observer of animals, a founder of the field of Animal Behavior. In his book *On Aggression,* where his principal subject is war and its relationship to aggression, the only chapters where we actually see females in any detail tend to be those where he describes the behavior of his beloved geese.

When he turns to consider aggression and war and how these relate to humans, we once again find no male/female distinctions. His discussion is entirely in terms of "man," and "men," and "humanity," and one is left to infer that whatever is true of men as a group is true of women as a group. We are left to assume that the biological agendas and priorities of the human sexes are the same.

I eagerly absorbed Christopher Boehm's *Hierarchy in the Forest*, a study of egalitarian cultures worldwide. But he consciously makes the same oversimplification. Early in the book he said he realized that males and females were quite different, but he nevertheless found it "easier to average any sex differences that exist and to treat human nature as a single entity" (p. 15). "My last chapter," he writes, "will be devoted to human nature, with a focus on its expression in males (p. 147)."

It is an unfortunate decision not to ask what females in the various cultures he described were doing. Did the women in this culture or that culture, for example, have control over essential resources? I would predict that this resource-controlling factor would critically affect their ability to exercise power to regulate the "upstart males" he was interested in.

It's quite possible that a female investigator looking at these many cultures might have chosen to take note of which sex controlled which resources. Books like *Feminism and Evolutionary Biology: Boundaries, Intersections, and Frontiers* edited by Patricia Gowaty and *Has Feminism Changed Science?* by Londa Schiebinger are among many on the subject of how the infusion of science with women has enriched many fields.

It's not that women necessarily do science differently from men. Although some have argued that women, in general, do have a significantly different mental approach. They argue that this affects not only the problems the sexes pick, but how they phrase the questions to be answered and their state of mind as they work. And that women, in general, have a more cooperative rather than controlling attitude to their subject.

In any case, one of the great beauties of the scientific method is that, in the end, the result has no race, no religion, no nationality, and no sex. So long as individuals ask the same questions, they will, maybe not initially but in the end, come up with the same answers. What seems to be the case is that the focus of the attention of men and women may differ because of differences in their life experiences.

When it comes to the subject of peace and war, we suffer from the severe blind spot that I call "hidden females." Consider this example: When asked on television soon after the September 11, 2001 disaster of the World Trade Center and Pentagon what he thought was the cause of the conflict, John Leo of U.S. News and World Report said it was a cultural war between the modern world and "people who have not been able to accept modernity." To be more accurate and to give clarity to his point, he would better have described it as between the modern world and *men* who have not been able to accept modernity. There were, after all, no women at the levers of power in the organization of Osama bin Laden.

Asked at about the same time on CNN's "Novak, Hunt, and Shields" if the United States government had a long-term strategy designed to solve the problem with Afghanistan, Senator Joseph Biden stressed that he felt the government was very concerned to make sure that both the northern and southern elements (that is, the tribes/warlords residing in those areas) of Afghanistan were represented in the final solution. He made no mention that the interests of Afghan women must be represented. Over 50% of the Afghan population remained invisible. From these statements, one is left to assume that women were in no way considered crucially pivotal to a strategy for ensuring the future of Afghan stability.

Chris Hedges vividly describes the narcotic allure of war in *War is a Force that Gives Us Meaning*. But who is "us?" His index does not even have an entry for "women." Are we simply to assume that war is equally compelling and meaningful to women?

When ex-president Clinton finished the speech I mentioned in the Preface, and I was reflecting on what he'd said and what he'd left out, I found myself wondering if this intelligent, widely-read man was unaware of this critical difference in the preference for domination or for win-win tendencies of the sexes. And it quickly struck me that such a thing was highly unlikely. The difference has simply been too well documented. And I suddenly suspected his omission more likely occurred because the social climate remains such that it would be embarrassingly unfashionable for such a powerful male to call on the world to empower its women.

My goal, then, is to have some part in changing our social climate so all who study and long for peace will readily acknowledge the long-term futility of trusting in male-dominated systems: that powerful leaders will loudly, urgently, and unfailingly insist on the inclusion of women as equal participants in all levels of social decision-making.

If we continue to fail to make a distinction between male and female agendas, between male and female inclinations, we will continue to perpetuate the mistaken idea that war lies at the feet of "people" rather than power-seeking or disaffected males. And unless we know and acknowledge the root cause of the affliction of war, we cannot hope to discover, invoke, or create a cure.

Francis Fukuyama's *The End of History and the Last Man*

Political scientist Francis Fukuyama wrote an enlightening and useful work entitled *The End of History and the Last Man*. His point is that history is moving, albeit in fits and starts, toward universal liberal democracy. He describes other forms of government, from kingships to communism to fascism, and describes the internal conditions that caused them to fall.

What does he mean by "the end of history?" At some point, he argues, people will arrive at a political system that meets the most basic need of the most people. That system will be stable, wars will cease, and there will be no more changes, violent or otherwise, to other systems—thus we will have reached the end of history.

Fukuyama had been a deputy director of the U.S. State Department's Policy and Planning Staff. In 1992, when his book was published, he was a consultant at the RAND think tank in Washington, D. C. Here is a man who has given considerable time to the issue of human social systems and their relation to war and to the end of war. But while his analysis is a strong one, it did not go far enough and falls significantly short in two ways.

Before considering these problem areas, note that *The End of History* suffers substantially because Fukuyama excludes almost all tribal or community-based societies from consideration. These societies, too, have been evolving all these millennia. But he focuses on the state-level, warring civilizations that are so central to the prevailing historical perspective. This is too narrow a view, because male and female behavior in state-level societies does not represent the full range of human potential when it comes to ways to organize our lives. As a result, Fukuyama is left to consider many examples of male use of power and few or none of female use of power. As a consequence, he fails to address the relevance of women's priorities and abilities to any ultimate "end of history."

Two Engines of History *The Scientific Method*

The Scientific Method

Nevertheless, Fukuyama has much to offer this discussion. He argues that two exceedingly powerful forces are at work in human history. The first force is quite recent, relatively speaking, and I fully agree with its profound significance. This is the introduction, roughly 300 years ago, of the scientific method. The introduction of the scientific method has led to what Fukuyama calls the "logic of modern science," and he argues that it drives us toward the establishment, at the end of history, of liberal democracies around the world.

How? The scientific method allows us to figure out how the world really works as opposed to how ancient philosophies or religions think it works. This method has flung open the door to heretofore unimagined technologies that have changed our lives in profound ways.

Most people would shudder at the thought of retreating to a past time where we lived in relative ignorance, pain, and want. Few people desire to emigrate to Afghanistan or Tanzania rather than to the United States or Denmark. In order to use and continue to develop those technologies, however, a society must continually produce a highly educated middle class. And the educated people of this middle class will not settle, over the long run, to be governed by any system other than a liberal democracy.

The Need For Recognition

But why should educated folks prefer democracy? Fukuyama's answer, inherited from Hegel, is his second powerful driving force, "the need for recognition."

Philosophers from Plato to Nietzsche have given the need for recognition different names. Fukuyama adopts Plato's word *thymos,* which roughly translates to "spiritedness," but he points out it refers to what others call desire for glory, pride or vainglory, love of fame, and ambition. Konrad Lorenz referred to this spirit when, in *On Aggression,* he described "militant enthusiasm." As a biologist, I consider it a desire for status and the power and advantages status brings – in short, "power-seeking."

As described by Fukuyama, all men have thymos (and presumably women), but some men (and presumably women like Cleopatra) display megalothymos—an excess of "spiritedness." It is megalothymos that, according to Fukuyama, is responsible for most wars. I call it "out-of-control, unchecked power-seeking." It appears to be an overwhelmingly male phenomenon; men willing to kill or have others kill for them to achieve dominance of their world, be it a small tribal one or a global one. I call them hyper-alpha males. Women also seek power, but historically they have been less likely to launch a community into war to achieve it.

Fukuyama continues by pointing out that humans are more than just economic machines that seek only to meet their needs for food, shelter, and sex. We are feeling beings. And he cites the various previously mentioned philosophers to bolster the argument that it is this need for recognition, this primary need of mankind, that a stable social system must meet. Further, according to Fukuyama, the liberal democracy, where all men are theoretically considered to be of equal worth and in fact have an equal vote, is the system that best fulfills that need for the maximum number of people.

Hence, when the world is full of liberal democracies, he argues, we will have reached stability at last, and history—at least in terms of never-ending experiments with different social systems—will come to a halt.

A Critique of Fukuyama's Hypothesis

Hidden Females

My first difficulty with Fukuyama's analysis is that, like so many before him, he suffers from a severe case of hidden females.

- Repeatedly when he uses the word humanity or humans or people he speaks of "mankind" in a way that leads readers to assume that what is characteristic of men is also characteristic of women. We are not sure he makes any distinction between mankind and woman-kind, since the latter is not mentioned.
- When he describes the struggle for "recognition," he claims that out of this struggle came "the relationship of lordship and bondage in all of its various manifestations, and the moral codes that arose out of it—the deference of a subject to his monarch, the peasant to his landlord, the haughty superiority of the aristocrat and so forth (p. 214)." But he doesn't mention female subordination to men. Again Fukuyama seems to have forgotten half of the human race.
- When he talks of the failure of an ancient democracy (Athens) to endure, he cites as one reason for their failure that they didn't guarantee freedom of speech, as illustrated by their execution of Socrates. Presumably Fukuyama considers this is a highly significant factor. Yet he fails to consider that women, potentially the most stabilizing force in their community, were not allowed a voice. Not in Athens or any other "democracies" or "republics" of the ancient world. In civic or state affairs, over one half of the people in these communities, those most inclined to social stability, were ignored. Surely this fact is at least equally as worthy of consideration as freedom of speech as a major reason for ultimate failure.

Until our major thinkers begin to consider both halves of the human equation in their speculations and analyses, until females are hidden no more, we will not arrive at the full picture of human life any more than we were able to do for baboons or gulls. Nor will we be likely to find a cure for what ails us.

The Need for Connectedness (Positively Met) and the End of History

So how can we reach an end to history, a place where the turmoil of revolt and war lies in our past and our creativity and energy can be wholeheartedly devoted to positive pursuits? Where I disagree most strongly with Fukuyama is in his acceptance of the proposition that, in order for history to end, it is the fundamental human "need for recognition" that must be met.

Humans have several fundamental needs: food, shelter, and protection being by far the most basic. We also have the need for sex, which can be sublimated but only with difficulty and with questionable, sometimes remarkably harmful, results to society and to individuals.

We *do* have a need for recognition. We inherit from our primate ancestors a form of social 'beingness that is most certainly bound up in dominance/power relationships of complex sorts. Men and women form dominance hierarchies and rigorously protect their status. Study after study shows that both sexes are highly sensitive, at every moment, to their relative status within their group. We desire that others acknowledge our worth/status, and given the freedom to do so, we strive to improve our status and level of recognition—our level of power.

But one need is far more critical. This is the "need for connectedness." I suggest here, most strongly, that *this* is the need that must be met, and in positive ways, if we are ever to achieve social stability that delivers the most profound human fulfillment.

Women, Power, and the Biology of Peace

What is a "need for connectedness?" I repeat, humans are social primates to the core. In the state of nature in which we evolved, a lone human being was a dead human being. Our most critical need from the moment of birth is to be connected (bonded) to our primary caregiver, whether that is our natural mother or some caregiver who steps into that role. Nor could our ancestors have survived or reproduced successfully without *belonging* to a group.

So critical is connectedness to survival and breeding that nature has endowed us with a deep psychic hunger for connection that is as important as the need for food and shelter. When we *belong,* we feel good, we feel right, we feel secure. We have the prospect of happiness (although no guarantee). When we are alone, we feel insecure, unsure, bereft, abandoned. When isolated and alone, most people sink into deep psychic pain.

When discussing the essentials necessary for people to heal emotionally after suffering through a disaster like the destruction of the World Trade Center, Dr. Sandra Bloom said that the most critical ingredient is "to remain *connected* to other people—not to withdraw (emphasis mine)." People who live into ripe old age are usually those who remain connected to family and community. Psychological counselors know that to avoid depression, even suicide, it is critical for a person to remain in contact with family and community.

When they face imminent death, high status achievers often realize that what matters most is not what they have done or what more they might do or how many strangers admire them or defer to them. What truly matters is the people they love and who love them, the people to whom they are connected.

One of the great solaces of religion is that it brings a sense of connectedness to something or someone vastly powerful; for people who have become disconnected from family, friends, and community, religion may provide their only sense of connectedness. Even those who have sought solitude in wilderness places describe the profound, positive joy of feeling *connected* to the planet and its creatures.

The need for connectedness will be satisfied, if not positively then negatively. Young people so need a connection to their parents that they will often endure astonishing abuse rather than leave or betray these adults. A woman may need a sense of connectedness so desperately that she will remain with a man who beats her. Young men who have become disconnected from their family are vulnerable candidates for gang membership so that they can "belong." Any male who is frustrated and disaffiliated from his family and community is ripe pickings for extremist groups that offer him belonging.

The "need for recognition" certainly has been hugely important as a motivator for the males of the state-level societies considered by Fukuyama. The "need for connectedness," though, is even more fundamental for humans, male or female, in order to be content with the status they achieve, whether that status is that of a dominant, equal or lowly subordinate. Until social systems function to ensure that most members satisfy their need for connectedness in positive ways, discontent will persist and the end of history will remain unachieved.

Fukuyama comes close to grasping this point when he questions whether the recognition one receives as a citizen of a large, contemporary democracy is necessarily more satisfying than the recognition people used to receive as members of small, tightly-knit, pre-industrial, agricultural (non-democratic) communities. His answer is an implicit, No. Unfortunately, he doesn't go on to make the link to a critical need for connectedness.

Similarly, at the end of his book, Fukuyama wonders whether, even if we achieve liberal democracies, they will be stable. Essentially he asks whether we will be satisfied even when we finally have all the material goods we require and political and social recognition as a worthy individual equal to other individuals. In view of the fact that the democracies and republics of the past failed to endure, he's quite right to be leery, as I am, that democracy by itself will guarantee long-term stability.

He notes that all other social systems (kingships, communism, totalitarianism, fascism) eventually collapsed or were overthrown because some inherently unresolvable contradiction left them vulnerable. Is there, he asks, some inherent contradiction in liberal democracies we can't anticipate or that we aren't recognizing that will bring on their demise as well?

One possible inherent contradiction seems almost self-evident to me. While a handful of liberal democracies are at least approaching sexual equality in decision-making, the vast majority remain woefully far from that condition. They are liberal democracies in name only since women are enfranchised in name only, participating mainly as tokens or exceptions. Few women actually vote. Fewer still hold state-level political offices.

In these token liberal democracies, the full force of female inclinations is unable to make a difference. So long as the male urge for recognition that is megalothymia is not checked by an equal force equally deeply rooted in our biology (namely the strong female desire for social stability), "liberal democracies" will remain vulnerable to the agitations of every world-conquering charismatic who utters the words for conquest in the right way.

And until the need for connectedness is met in positive ways, even true liberal democracies will live with a contradiction between what people would like to feel and what they actually do feel. They will live with contradiction as the pleasure, joy, fulfillment, delight, and other positive emotions that come from positive connectedness with others and the planet that sustains us are inadequately filled by the grim, negative, and unsatisfying substitutes that fill the emotional void when connectedness is found in negative ways.

Certainly this critical need applies with equal significance to the men who by temperament are the most likely to be agitators for war. The men most likely to rouse others who are also unsatisfied and unfulfilled to join them in war.

Women, Power, and the Biology of Peace

In a will discovered in his suitcase, Mohamad Atta, one of the terrorists who participated in the destruction of the World Trade Center in September, 2001, wrote:

I don't want any woman to go to my grave at all... I don't want a pregnant woman or a person who is not clean to say goodbye...

How sad... and how revealing from this man quite ready to kill innocents and himself. So long as men and women are estranged from each other, so long as they are unequal and one is considered subservient, so long as men continue to be estranged from satisfying, joy-giving connections to their children, so long as humans are alienated from the natural world and instead consider themselves its masters and dominators, the need for deep connectedness will remain unmet. Discontent will generate strife, the outlet for which traditionally has been war. We will continue to have an itch that somehow must be scratched.

We have a long way to go before we are fully, positively connected. The hard work of trial and error, discovery and implementation, required to achieve that goal is the challenge before us, the challenge of Waging Peace.

Looking for Guidance

I've often been struck by the irony that we surprisingly often look for advice on the human condition and what drives and satisfies us by referring to "experts" or "geniuses" who are disaffected or dysfunctional males—males who often do not know the joys of family, parenting, immersion in community, or oneness with nature, males who are convinced women should be submissive to them. Surely this is folly.

In Fukuyama's book I found new examples of this strange blindness. He, for example, selects such thinkers as Plato, Aristotle,

Paschal, and Nietzsche as important contributors to understanding humans and history.

Well, Aristotle felt that women weren't quite fully human. One can only wonder how that assumption affected the philosophy he developed that influenced so many leaders in the centuries that followed, and even today.

The portraits Fukuyama draws of Paschal and Nietzsche are stunningly chilling. These men have profoundly influenced what our best and brightest have pondered as they sought to solve the world's problems. Fukuyama notes that Pascal secluded himself in a monastery when he was thirty-one. "He strapped nails to the chair he sat on when people came to visit him. If he felt he was getting any pleasure in the talk, he'd push himself against the nails. In his last four years he could not communicate with people at all."

Nietzsche's "fingers turned blue in the winter because he refused to heat his room." In the years before he went insane, "scarcely a day in ten passed without his experiencing terrible headaches." In one bit of writing, Nietzsche assessed family life as, "...messy, clinging, and of an annoying and repetitive pattern, like bad wallpaper." Here was a man who seems hugely disconnected and, given his philosophy, probably without much lasting or genuine joy.

These are our authorities?

Not all influential thinkers have come to dismissive conclusions about women. We don't know sufficient details of the family or personal life of Plato to know how they might have shaped his thinking, but the view he expressed in *The Laws* and some other writings reflects a notable respect for women, a view remarkably lacking notions of subjugation or inferiority:

> Nothing can be more absurd than the practice that prevails in our country of men and women not following the same pursuits with all their strength and with one mind, for thus, the state, instead of being whole, is reduced to half.

Women, Power, and the Biology of Peace

I would like to know how Plato arrived at his opinions. I'd especially be curious about the nature of his relationships with women, beginning with his mother and sister, and how those relationships influenced him—what kind of connectedness he had with women during his formative years. I'd like to be able to see into his personal life and the relationships he had with others to know if he lived dismally or positively.

Where should we look for help today? We should certainly start with the scientific method to find out what kind of animal we truly are as opposed to what armchair philosophers think we should be or what we like to think we are. Only when we separate fact from fiction can we be guided toward solutions that will actually work—that is, stable solutions. What we'll find, I suggest, is what truly wise ones already have found: that connectedness, positively met, is where joy and fulfillment lie. And with them will come stability.

What to Do with Young Men?

The most disruptive sector of any society is likely to be its young males. Restlessness and aggressiveness are obvious in little boys more than in little girls at even very early ages. With the onset of testosterone flow at puberty, the male hunger for status and recognition is fed new fuel.

Young men who have failed to become positively connected or who seek connectedness in negative ways are especially disruptive. Martin Daly and Margo Wilson, in *Homicide,* looked across cultures and document the negative, aggressive influence of young males, something they have called "The Young Male Syndrome."

According to Nyborg, in *Hormones, Sex and Society,* roughly half of America's violent crimes are committed by young males under the age of twenty-four, the age at which male testosterone levels peak. In an article in *Newsweek,* Fareed Zakaria points out that Arab countries are experiencing a massive youth bulge, with 25 % of their populations being under the age of 25. Zakaria goes on to argue, citing the French and 1979 Iranian revolutions, that "when populations are faced with large numbers of restless young males and this is combined with even slight economic and political change, the society can easily fall prey to revolutionary activities."

Some cultures and subcultures strongly discourage male aggression (e.g., the American Quaker subculture, North American Hopi, the !Kung San, see also PeacefulSocieties.org and Fry 2006, 2007). Warrior cultures encourage it. Their preoccupation with aggression, war, and guns seems almost boundless.

The strong attraction of young men to violence is often exploited by such a society and by subgroups within it. In the United States, for example, consider how Hollywood tailors the violence of action films to the youthful male audience it seeks to attract. Or step into a video game parlor where young, would-be warriors engage in virtual battles with every imaginable enemy. You'll find few young girls in the room. American entrepreneurs seeking to draw women into computer games have had a hard time, since most games are essentially aggressive shoot-'em-up or smash 'em scenarios.

Given that thymos runs high in most young males, many cultures have, nevertheless, found positive ways to tame and direct those restless urges. How do peaceful societies deal with their young men? How do they assure their young men that they are an important and valued part of their community? Many put young males through demanding initiations, rites of passage into manhood. For that matter, many cultures also initiate girls.

The mythologist Joseph Campbell is often quoted as saying, "Boys everywhere have a need for rituals marking passage to manhood. If society doesn't provide them, they will inevitably invent their own." When a young man in a culture having rites of passage has completed his challenge or test, he knows he is a man. And his community officially recognizes him as such, a part of fulfilling his need for recognition. The community also embraces him as a worthy adult, fulfilling his critical need for connectedness. Appropriate initiation by the adults of a young man's community, initiation that includes guidance and caring, can inoculate against seeking connectedness in negative ways.

Liberal democracies have no official equivalent testing and honoring of youth. Rites of passage are something most secular societies have lost. A year of service, in the community or perhaps elsewhere in the world, one that included an official **testing and reward for success,** would help set young males on a positive path. A hard test, one that involves courage, discipline, creativity and doing something constructive for the community and which once accomplished brings a profound sense of pride, is critical. Simply spending time would not be enough.

Growing numbers of scholars and agencies are recognizing this need for a modern rite of passage. In a search of the internet, for example, I found The Journey program in Pretoria, South Africa and the Animus Vision Quest of the Animus Valley Institute in Durango, Colorado. Boston University's *The Daily Free Press* reported that the Bill and Melinda Gates Foundation provided a $5.4 million grant to Boston area YouthBuild USA. YouthBuild programs help undereducated youths ages 16-24 work toward high school diplomas as they build houses, in collaboration with Habitat for Humanity, for homeless and low-income people. While not in itself a formal rite of passage, this is the kind of program, if presented appropriately and the young people honored appropriately, could provide both young men and young women with that vital sense of community belonging.

Controlling aggression in positive ways to achieve social stability means we need to exert focus on young men. But such service should involve youths of both sexes because both sexes have much to contribute. And to develop connectedness, both young men and young women need to know that their community expects them to give back as a part of a shared human bond. Young women—the hands that will rock cradles of the future—also need to learn what is expected of them.

For society to ignore this particular "initiation" need of its young is astonishingly shortsighted. Since we know that developing positive connectedness to one's community is a critical component of wholesome development, failing to expend time, money, and creative resources to meet this youthful need is also morally bankrupt.

Meaningful work that brings meaningful reward is also critical to ward off disaffection. Young males who cannot find such work suffer lack of respect, from themselves and others. They become hostile. Discontent from many such young men leads to instability, usually with tragic consequences in crime or even revolt and war.

If a community finds that jobs for its youth are lacking, the adults must consider it their solemn responsibility to convene with urgency to tackle this problem. They should call in experts. They should seek out all available resources and examples from communities that have conquered this challenge. They should not rest until they have provided avenues to meaningful employment. They should attack this problem with the focused passion—and money—they would muster if they were at war and were devising means to halt a deadly enemy invasion or terrorist attack—because for a young person and his or her community, lack of meaningful work that promises a meaningful future *is* a deadly enemy.

Moving from "Win-Lose" Cultures to Cultures of "Mutual Gain"

I indicated earlier that another likely necessary condition for a culture to evolve to state-level without warfare would be an ethos that rejects violence, so that when conflicts arise, violent means of resolution are soundly rejected. We are unlikely to create a more peaceful world unless we embrace a deep and abiding commitment to non-violent conflict resolution. In the language of negotiation, we must move away from a "win-lose" approach to life and passionately embrace a "mutual gain" (win-win) approach.

Women, Power, and the Biology of Peace

How, then, can we move from where most of us are, steeped in win-lose mentality, to where we need to be? Debra Tannen's book, *The Argument Culture: Stopping America's War of Words*, is a study of a warrior culture in which, in her view, the level of aggression in the public sphere is rising.

After describing examples of conflict, the book explores ways for Americans to move beyond argument to understanding and harmony. She looks at other cultures and how they deal with conflicts ("Listening to Other Cultures" and "It Takes a Village to Settle Disputes"). In her last chapter, she describes how we could move from a "debate" mentality, in which two sides are in opposition and the goal is to win, to a "dialogue" mentality, where many different sides present their views, all of which are considered and given due reflection.

Anthropologist William Ury argues in *Getting to Peace: Transforming Conflict at Home, at Work, and in the World* that war in state-level societies is primarily the result, along with several other factors, of a failure of ancient, or tribal, systems of negotiating conflicts. Those were processes that involved what he calls a Third Side. That is, third parties served as mediators, facilitators, referees, arbiters, teachers, and so on. In the second half of his book, he presents a clear and compelling account of how the modern ethos of conflict resolution in complex societies must be changed if we are to decrease or eliminate warfare. He provides practical suggestions for how to achieve that goal using the Third Side. Along with other challenges already described, this goal of changing our conflict-resolving ethos will be a critical ingredient in waging peace.

I take the massive demonstrations by thousands around the world against a unilateral American invasion of Iraq and the desire for peaceful Iraqi disarmament as a significant positive sign that large parts of the worldwide human community are embracing the non-violence ethos. To succeed in actually bringing about peaceful stability, though, the world's important players on *all* sides must agree to unequivocally reject armed aggression. We've not yet arrived at that happy state. Some leaders continue to lust for glory of conquest and domination and their unchecked urges continue to torment us as we seek to contain them.

Anticipating Problems

A skillful mother anticipates problems looming ahead of her family and finds ways to head them off or to resolve them before they can do harm. Natural selection has honed this female skill called prospience over countless generations. In *The First Sex*, Fisher cites studies showing that women CEOs are, in general, more inclined than male CEOs to habitually look forward, which enables them to anticipate where problems may arise. They use this forward-looking habit to get ahead of the potential conflict curve. Looking forward to defuse potential problems is part of the win-win, make nice, keep-the-peace tendencies of our female heritage, another reason why we need to harness female inclinations for the public sphere.

While this talent may characterize females in general, men who are good leaders are certainly just as skilled at anticipating problems. To reach a satisfying end of history, it will be the task of all our leaders, of both sexes, to think proactively and creatively to uncover the seeds of social unrest and implement programs to prevent them from sprouting.

Environmentalists doubtless hope for similarly visionary leaders who will care for our planet's future. Without them, we may so seriously alter the environment in ways hostile to our well-being that our history may end quite brutally despite our best social and political efforts to achieve peace. The issue of peace will no longer be relevant.

Empowering Women

Worldwide movements are already focused on empowering women because, "Women's rights are human rights." This was part of

Women, Power, and the Biology of Peace

the concluding statement of the 1995 Fourth World Conference on Women.

Individuals who can make a difference have also embraced change. Oprah Winfry, arguably America's single most influential woman as I write, donated funds in South Africa for the Oprah Winfry Leadership Academy For Girls. One girl is quoted by the LA Times as saying, "We are looking for strong, brave girls with heart. I believe girls are going to take over the world. Men have been in control long enough but don't worry, we're prepared to share power." I wasn't there, but I imagine this comment being accompanied by Oprah's warm, embracing smile.

The American Secretary of State, Colin Powell, provided another notable example in an address on November 19, 2001. Barely over two months after the statement of Senator Biden that appeared to take no heed of Afghan women, Secretary Powell said, "The rights of the women of Afghanistan will not be negotiable." Here was formal recognition of a growing sense that leaving women out of the power loop is not only not moral, it's not smart.

Powell was speaking of the position of the United States as she, her allies, the United Nations, and the people of Afghanistan drew up reconstruction plans. Poor, ravaged Afghanistan is a classic example of a country that has long embraced traditions of female suppression and male-led warfare. If Secretary Powell's words prove prophetic and Afghan women are given full rights, including the right to vote and to receive education, the future of Afghanistan is likely to be both fascinating and enlightening. The country will be what scientists call a "natural experiment," a living laboratory we could not morally or practically create but one from which we can learn.

What changes might the unleashing of the female within a democratic (egalitarian) context bring to this starkly patriarchal people? If the empowerment of Afghan women is treated not as just desirable, but necessary to success, what will happen? Will we see a trend, however tentative, toward win-win conflict resolution and compromise rather than endless battles? On the other hand, if women are kept "in their place," will the country achieve long-term social stability nevertheless? Over four thousand years of history and the facts I have presented here predict that the answer in that case is: No.

Empowerment Beyond the Political

To halt war, female empowerment must ultimately embrace the totality of women's lives. In the western democracies, for example, women enjoy a variety of rights and they wield ever-increasing influence as the result of changes accumulated slowly over generations.

For developing countries, giving women the vote is but a first step. Giving *only* the vote will not prevent the eventual incorporation of and expression of the female preference for stability, but it will slow the process dramatically, dragging it out over generations. Simultaneously changing other aspects of women's lives when they are given the vote will accelerate the process.

A few moments of reflection and most people realize that if we are to hasten transformation to a world that rejects war, plans well ahead for problems, and fosters satisfying connectedness, women's empowerment must include educational, economic, legal, and religious changes, as well as the political one. And it must be worldwide.

Education

Meaningful empowerment begins with wide and deep education. Without this, most women will continue to buy into all the old familiar ways. They will not recognize even that change is possible, and they'll be unlikely to know how best to vote in order to bring about appropriate change. After all, we must not ever forget that women have collaborated with men in virtually every human endeavor so far, including war.

Women are "the hand that rocks the cradle" and thus they supposedly rule the world. There is truth in this phrase. Who bound the feet of girl children in China? Not men. In cultures that exposed newborn girls to die, who did the exposing? Not men, but rather a mid-wife or perhaps the grandmother. Who performed, and still does perform, operations on little girls so they cannot experience pleasure in sex as an adult? Until the recent introduction of modern medicine and clinics, it wasn't men.

Women in every generation have proudly sent sons they nursed off to war after war.

Why have women been so willing to collaborate in so many ways in their own degradation and the loss of their sons? Well, women are not saints. And they have been as much constrained by their biology as men, only in different ways. The need to reproduce successfully, by whatever means possible, has been the driving force in their evolution and behavior as well as the evolution and behavior of men (see Hrdy's *Mother Nature*). When they find themselves without power, as they have been in so many cultures, women do the best they can. For too many millennia, the "best they can" was a rule that reads much like, "Get as close as you can to the most powerful male you can and keep in the good graces of the males that run the system." The result has been collaboration with males in ways that reinforced male-dominated systems.

Instead of reinforcing patriarchies, politically empowered and *educated* women, fully participating in a liberal democracy, can be a potent catalyst for change and social stability.

Economics

Not only is meaningful empowerment educational, it must also be economic. Without economic security, women cannot afford to take the risk of stepping out to insist that things change—or to recruit others to vote and act with them. Only economic independence can free women from the need to collaborate. (Appendix 1 is a list of organizations, e.g. Village Banking Program and Heifer Foundation, working to give women economic independence.) Riane Eisler's *The*

Read *Wealth of Nations* offers us a view of a new economic system based on care-giving, one that values women's work.

The Laws

Empowerment must also be legal. Legal empowerment is particularly important with respect to divorce when divorce is possible, ensuring that women have access to their children and an equitable sharing of family assets. Beyond these two most critical areas, laws must guarantee equal rights and responsibilities in all areas of life: equal pay for equal work, equal access to job training, legal protections against spousal abuse.

The list of needed laws is long, and a society must be committed to seeing that they are enforced. Laws not enforced are worse than useless because they hide the reality of continuing inequality.

Religion

Empowerment must also be religious. Without religious empowerment women will be silenced in the critical realm that molds our world view of what is right and what is possible. For traditional religions that have taught that women are to remain strictly in the home, change will come slowly and will be difficult. Change will come last in this sphere of life because religious tradition is extraordinarily resistant to change.

As women become empowered in education and wealth, however, their newly acquired position will exert pressure on their religions. Liturgy will be affected, for example, as women seek affirmation of something feminine in the divine. Even now, in some liberal American denominations one can find prayers that begin, "To God, our Father and Mother." On February 2, 2002, in an article entitled "New Bible Edition to be Gender-Neutral," the Los Angeles Times reported that the evangelical publisher Zondervan and the International Bible Society will publish a new edition of the Bible in which, for example, "Sons of God" will become "children of God."

Women, Power, and the Biology of Peace

Some women may be expected to reject patriarchal religions altogether and find the answers they seek in New Age religions or perhaps movements like the goddess-worshipping Wicca. One of the most startling examples of change in the United States is that, after centuries of tradition of a male priesthood, there is a battle among Catholics over whether to ordain women as priests. Reform and Conservative branches of Judaism now have significant numbers of women rabbis. While Orthodox Judaism does not yet accept women as rabbis, in America the age-old practice of separating women in synagogues has all but disappeared. Many protestant denominations in the United States also struggle with women's ordination even though there are precedents for it going back to at least 1852, when the Congregationalist Church ordained Antoinette Brown.

If the collective wisdom comes to believe that it ought to be considered right and possible that women are equal to men in social and civic affairs, religion must, and will, eventually affirm that women are considered equal by whatever power they consider divine. If religion doesn't evolve to match a public commitment to equality for the sexes, we would be teaching children a message contrary to public practice. While such a conflict between practice and belief can persist for a time, it is unlikely to be permanent.

Worldwide

And finally, empowerment must be worldwide. As mentioned earlier, peace cannot occur when only some cultures embrace an unswerving commitment to non-violent conflict resolution. All parties must be in agreement that force of arms will be rejected. Empowering women in some cultures but not others is unlikely to bring a stable world. Unless changed from within, cultures that are now patriarchal and steeped in the tradition of violence and war will continue to value and use, even celebrate, force.

As already stated, the two factors most likely to bring about worldwide change are the introduction of democracy, which decentralizes power, and women's suffrage and education, which will gradually decrease the tendency to choose the option of fighting. Organizations and individuals focused on the goal of global peace are keenly aware of this and are allocating their resources in places where help can have the greatest impact (Appendix 1).

Predicting The Future

How long will all this take? Is it really possible to change the world as it has been for so many millennia?

If the democracies survive and women keep the vote, change is inevitable. It can't be stopped. It may take several generations, but it will happen. Empowered women can and will change the world. If democracies do not persist, then, as they say, all bets are off.

The question really is: will we make the transition to sufficient female empowerment swiftly enough? The future may instead witness the loss of democracy and a return to some new form of political or religious authoritarianism. Perhaps we will slip into a new Dark Age.

The people of Germany, for example, freely elected Hitler. While it seems highly improbable, nothing guarantees that the United States will not vote itself into an authoritarian theocracy such as that envisioned by its religious right. Or perhaps humanity will blunder into a clash with nuclear, chemical, or biological devastation, with the cultural makeup of the ultimate survivor/winner being quite beyond prediction.

It's not at all unreasonable to feel uneasy, to feel a profound sense of urgency. And this book does not even touch on perilous ecological changes we are precipitating, seemingly without thought to their potentially dire long-term consequences as male-dominated industries continue their quest for profit and the overall population continues to burgeon and burden habitats as ever more *Homo sapiens* compete for resources.

It is a cliché, but true nonetheless: you are either part of the solution or part of the problem. You are a woman who votes, or one who thinks her voice is not important. You are a woman who educates herself about life and how you might participate in making it better, or you accept that what always has been is what always will and should be. You are a man who has figured out on your own the civilizing influence of women and supports them as they struggle for equality, or you are a man who has decided you prefer a world in which women stay in their place. You encourage young women to strive and achieve, or you put blocks in their way. Or maybe you just drag your feet.

Appendix 1 lists a sample of many organizations committed to the struggle for change leading to more balanced male/female participation worldwide. The website, *A Future Without War.org*, (see end of Appendix 1 for details) describes a strategy for abolishing war and provides links to hundreds of activist organizations. Appendix 2 suggests steps all individuals can take to be a part of needed change as we Wage Peace.

A World Full Of Empowered Women

It is impossible to predict what a world with fully empowered women might look like. Consider the profound changes in family structure and social life in Western democracies over the last hundred years. How many of those changes could have been predicted? Some of them. But only some of them.

From the experience of Western cultures, we know what many of the first steps look like. Many have already occurred. Laws are passed that guarantee women the right to an education; ensure that when a divorce occurs, women do not lose custody of their children and that an equitable share of any property goes to the women; ensure that women who do work equal to that of men are paid the same; and ensure that the legal system protects women from physical abuse. In a number of Western countries, women have had these legal protections long enough for effects on social structures to be felt, particularly in the structures of family and workplace.

Such legal changes lead to financial changes. As they work and accumulate property, women become more financially independent and, through application of their wealth, increasingly influence the products that are developed and sold, the entertainment that is sought and accepted, and the businesses that flourish.

We can also expect to see changes in sexual practices. The ideal of chastity before marriage may fall away. Also, women will increasingly expect to have as much pleasure in sex as the men who share their chamber. And fewer women are likely to find positive appeal in sexual jealousy as expressed by the concept that a woman "belongs" to a man.

As women pursue careers or work outside the home, patterns of childcare will change. Most modern women don't have access to the third-party care of an extended family, as was the case in so many cultures in the past. Because the welfare of their children is a prime concern, in the United States parents are currently between a rock and hard place because out-of-home childcare is often of questionable quality or is not accessible or both. Workplace laws are likely to be altered to allow longer maternal leave and flexible work schedules. More public resources will likely be devoted to determine what form of childcare is best, to determine the long term effects of out-of-home care on children, and to improve the quality and reliability of out-of-home care.

In 1906, Finnish women gained the right to vote (the first women in Europe, third in the world after New Zealand and Australia). They were the first women in the democratic world eligible for election. Only 95 years later, Finnish women are highly educated, 70% of married women work, maternity leave is nine months, part of which can be paternity leave, and close to half the members of the government are women.

The entire fabric of society is likely to be affected when women are fully empowered. For example, end-of-life care has historically been overwhelmingly the task of women. It still is much more often women nurses and family members who spend the long hours tending the dying—and watching them suffer. It is no coincidence that the founder of the modern Hospice movement was the British Dame Cicely Saunders (in America, Elizabeth Kubler-Ross is more well-known). Hospice care, with its acceptance of death as a natural part of life and a part of life that should be experienced without pain, is already a huge change in our approach to dying. As women gain influence, it is likely that laws regarding death with dignity without state interference will become the norm.

A particularly thoughtful discussion on this subject is that of Helen Fisher in *Anatomy of Love,* where she, too, argues that the agricultural tradition or "farm life" profoundly altered the relationship between the sexes. And she describes numerous ways modern life is coming to resemble our nomadic hunter-gatherer past:

> ...modern social trends...have come across the centuries, up from primitives who wandered onto the plains of Africa at least four million years ago...We are shedding the agricultural tradition and, in some respects, returning to our nomadic roots. Few of us still live in the house where we grew up...many of us have several places we call home—our parent's house, the office, our own residence, and perhaps a vacation spot. We migrate between them. We no longer grow our own food. We now hunt and gather in the grocery store and then carry home our catch...We commute to work again. And we have a loose network of friends and relatives, many of whom live far away.
> These are habits from our past.
> We are shedding the sexual attitudes of farm life too. In preindustrial Europe, a wedding often marked a merger of property and an alliance

between families. So marriage had to be stable and permanent. This necessity is gone. A woman's job was to bear her husband's seed and raise his young; hence our agrarian forerunners required virginity at marriage. This custom is gone. Many of our farming ancestors carefully arranged their marriages. This practice is largely gone. They banned divorce. This is gone. They had a double standard for adultery. This has changed. ...Vast numbers of women work outside the home. We have double-income families. We are more nomadic. And we have a growing equality between the sexes. In these respects, we are returning to traditions of love and marriage that are compatible with our ancient human spirit.

Fisher makes two important points. First, the changes happening now lie within the wide boundary of our human nature: we're not evolving into something new and different. Second, we are moving into a future that, ironically, has much in common with the ancient past.

No one knows what a future with empowered women worldwide will look like. But it will certainly look nothing like the world we know today—nothing. And because this is a major, all-embracing revolution, the trip is going to be a bumpy journey.

Blame And Choice

Who is to blame for war? The men who start and participate in them? The women who collaborate with and encourage the men?

Until recently, blame has been the wrong word, because it implies a knowledge we didn't possess. Not until the last two or three hundred years have we been able to make war an "informed" choice. Only in the aftermath of the scientific revolution have we had the capacity to understand what our ancestors would have considered irrepressible nature.

The scientific method is not only an engine driving human societies toward liberal democracies. The scientific method has changed

Women, Power, and the Biology of Peace

the moral landscape of war. Before we knew how to find out why we behave the way we do, we lived in a state of ignorance. Evolution, a blind and amoral process, had shaped us to want and need certain things in order to reproduce. We reacted to those wants and needs and justified them with laws and religions and customs. Our wants and needs came first. Laws, religions, and customs to regulate or rationalize our behavior came second.

In every society, individuals who survived the struggle to live and to reproduce were moved by their biological priorities. Matters such as the treatment of women, the fair distribution (or hoarding) of resources, and the challenges posed by young males (to create warriors or fashion men of peace) were decided by expedience rather than sure and certain knowledge of consequences. Humans followed the dictates of biology and did what worked best in a given time and place with particular sets of resources.

In the past, people of good will might come to different conclusions about the best way to organize society. Those who felt that subordinating women was best (Aristotle) could marshal their arguments. Those who felt the sexes should be treated equally (Plato) could marshal contrary argument. Everyone could and did build religions and customs to support one view or the other and often defied anyone to question their "clearly evident truths."

The scientific method allows us to replace ignorance of our species with knowledge. We have become informed. Blame now *is* a relevant word. We know why we behave as we do. We understand the root causes of wars. Knowing the causes, we also know that wars can be prevented.

We can and will debate how best to make necessary changes—how best to bring equality to women or hope to young men or a fair distribution of the earth's bounty to all her people. But we can no longer hide behind ignorance. A truly informed, and hence deeply moral choice is ours to make: we can do those things that foster war or those that foster peace.

Back To Balance

The Study of Existing Women-centered Cultures

What would the world be like if women ran it?

We have little material to study for hints. Fortunately, there exist a few remaining cultures where women are powerful and where the culture remains somewhat untouched by the western world—cultures that are strongly women-centered.

Drs. Peggy Reeves Sanday and Heide Göttner-Abendroth are interested in learning what such societies might teach us. They use the term *matriarchy*. I've explained earlier why I disagree with that term and why I think the absence of matriarchy in world history is significant. It suggests what the results might be if women were to be empowered, and it would not be the reverse of patriarchy. But whatever you call these cultures, matriarchies or women-centered, they are fascinating.

Sanday has spent years with the Minangkabau of West Sumatra, Indonesia and has written *Women at the Center: Life in a Modern Matriarchy*. The Minangkabau are matrilocal and the husband moves in with his wife's family. I quote from her web site at http://www.sas.upenn.edu~psanday/eggifemale.html:

> Women inherit the ancestral rice and farm lands along with the houses of the older women. Women manage the proceeds of the land, with the cooperation of their brothers and the senior males of their matrilineal clan.
>
> Conceived in Western terms, the Minangkabau matriarchate is best defined as 'mother right' not female rule. Neither male nor female rule is possible according to Minang social philosophy because of their belief that decision making should be by consensus. Although differences of opinion are regarded as normal, consensus is the goal of all deliberations. About differences of opinion the Minangkabau have a proverb: Crossing wood in the hearth makes the fire glow.

Women, Power, and the Biology of Peace

This notion of crossing wood is repeated in the idea that males and females complement one another—like the skin and nail of the fingertip—I was told. The consequence is a peaceable, nearly violence free society with a remarkable egalitarian philosophy undergirding the activities of everyday life.

Heidi Göettner-Abendroth's major work, *Matriarchy* (published in German as *Das Matriarchat*), is, as I write, still seeking an English publisher. She has devoted much of her time to the life of the Mosuo of China, non-Chinese people who live around Lake Lugu, surrounded by high mountain peaks not far from Tibet. A technical work about the entire complex of communities that constitute this culture is *A Society Without Fathers and Husbands* by Cai Hua. As the title suggests, what is perhaps most fascinating about the Mosuo is that they have no marriage. A woman lives with her family and chooses lovers who come to her to "visit" at night. During the day the men return to their own mother's (or grandmother's) lodgings for work.

Chet Lancaster has written *The Goba of the Zambezi: Sex Roles, Economics and Change,* another study of one of these women-centered cultures.

What can we learn from such people as the Minangkabau, Mosuo, and Goba?

The first question might be: are all their cultures in fact more peaceful? In a world where people are not isolated from others—by being alone on an island or perhaps nestled in their own Shangri-la, surrounded by virtually impenetrable mountains—remaining totally at peace is not a likely possibility. Aggressive neighbors have to be dealt with, one way or the other.

Cultural anthropologists Ember and Ember describe a fascinating pattern already detected cross-culturally relating to war. From the type of warfare practiced, we can predict whether residence will be matrilocal or patrilocal.

Women, Power, and the Biology of Peace

How does this work? As already noted, neighboring communities are often enemies. If the wars that break out between such groups are between people who speak the same language, it's called "internal warfare." If the wars are at least sometimes internal, residence is almost always patrilocal, not matrilocal.

In other societies, warfare is with speakers of other languages and never within the same society. This is "External warfare." When warfare is purely external, residence is almost always matrilocal.

Undoubtedly, numerous environmental and historical conditions underlie the development of patrilocal and matrilocal societies. But whatever may be the biological ultimate causes of matrilocality or patrilocality, a key factor used when making decisions about how to settle disputes appears to be whether the disputes are resolved "between us" or "between us and them." Female-centered cultures appear strongly inclined to accommodation instead of making war among "us."

We may continue to be conscious of our social, cultural, and racial differences, but thanks to technology, **Homo sapiens** now shares a growing and profound feeling that the world has become one global village. We are all "us." Even notable world leaders have some sense that success in avoiding wars over long periods depends on our ability to see ourselves as one. In his effort to disarm Iraq's Saddam Hussein, British Prime Minister Tony Blair, for example, urged the civilized world to unite behind "a new doctrine of international community."

Apparently women-centered cultures respond strongly and positively to the sense of avoiding wars among "us," something male centered cultures lack. Here is another indication that in our fight to be rid of wars, we are on the right track to tap into female inclinations.

Another question to ask of these women-centered cultures might be, how do men and women in women-centered cultures share power? What form of power sharing is most conducive to social stability and satisfying life?

Positive Aspects of Aggression

What would the world be like if women ran it and men were restricted to the home, locked in a male version of a harem? For hints about the answer to this question, we have no examples. None. Except in fiction and fantasy, such a state has never existed anywhere in human history.

But my strong gut instinct is that with the passage of time, such a world would be stultifying. We'd be strangled by an unchecked female inclination to social stability, subjected unrelentingly to the deeply seated desire to never rock the boat. We would lose the excitement that comes with innovation, restlessness, exploration, striving.

No one questions that males bring an abundance of positive things to the human equation, small things as well as great ones. It would be a great mistake to lock males away at home. What we think of as male energy has impelled us to venture out to explore the unknown, climb the highest peak, create the grandest building, push beyond just one more horizon, to invent the newest, most amazing gizmo.

We may one day find ways to eliminate the proximal causes of war and redirect aggressive urges entirely into positive endeavors (exploration, invention, sports, business), but the capacity for aggression is not going to disappear. Nor would we want it to! Konrad Lorenz's *On Aggression* can, in some respects, be considered a bit outdated, but the book remains an impressive review of animal behavior and its relationship to aggression. In his last chapter, "Avowal of Optimism," Lorenz writes that without aggression "the tackling of a task or problem, the self-respect without which everything a man does from morning till evening, from the morning shave to the sublimest artistic or scientific creations, would lose impetus; everything associated with ambition, ranking order, and countless other equally indispensable behavior patterns would probably also disappear... In the same way, a very important and specifically human faculty would probably disappear too: laughter." Any comedian understands at once how much of humor depends on a subtle, and sometimes not too subtle, expression of aggression.

Again from Lorenz: "The bonds of love and friendship, from which all kindness and charity springs and which represent the great antithesis to aggression" are, in fact, dependent on aggression. Psychologists have studied the tension of give and take, the conflicts engaged in and conflicts resolved that are inseparable from the formation of loving bonds. No marriage, no relationship between parents and children, no deeply rooted friendship is ever without conflict—**or the reconciliation after conflict that cements the bond.** We cannot afford to lose our aggressive instinct. We'd lose too many good things that are expressive of being human.

When women exhibit traits of daring and exploration—as they frequently do—we value those traits as something men in general bring to the dance of life. Balance is what we need, not one-dimensionality. We revere those of either sex who stretch the limits. It's just important that those who push the boundaries be restrained so that, in their enthusiasm, they don't step on or crush others such that social turmoil and riot or war results.

Balance

Most men do not love war. War games, perhaps. Planning war (or how to win), yes. But not actual war. This is especially true for men who have been in battle where they could feel the fear, engage the enemy, or see the bloody, broken bodies that are the result. Men who have been in battle, without exception, have told me they *hate* war.

Most men, if given a choice, would rather make love, not war. I find this extremely hopeful.

The problem is, and always has been, that some men thrive on war—particularly those megalothymic Alexanders, Caesars, Attilas, Genghis Khans, and Napoleons. Regrettably, other men, strongly predisposed to exciting group action and male bonding, too easily find themselves unable to resist the call to battle, honor, bonding, sacrifice and glory—the buzzwords used to summon the necessary followers.

The long history of wars of every form fought for every conceivable reason led by men from social structures of every imaginable kind demonstrates that it is impossible for men to help themselves. They cannot free themselves from the call to war. What is needed—the only thing likely to work and be stable—is to counter the inherited male inclination for group aggression with an equally unstoppable, equally deeply rooted female inclination for social stability.

When both male and female inclinations are encouraged simultaneously, male aggression will be bound by limits. Liberal democracies in which both sexes exercise the vote are the forums through which balance can be expressed. If we make changes with men and women in full democratic partnership, we can benefit from the best of what we think of as "male" and "female" traits to arrive at a balanced harmony. We can stop the regular sacrifice of lives and resources to the horseman, War. We can turn our attention and focused energies to the great challenge and rewards of Waging Peace.

Appendix I

Organizations Dedicated to Empowering Women Worldwide

Women's Resources on the Web

About.com: Women's Issues: Third World
http://womensissues.about.com

United States Information Agency: Resources for Women
http://usinfo.state.gov/topical/global//women/woman.htm

Women's Human Rights Net
http://www.whrnet.org/home.htm

Women's Human Rights Resources
http://www.law-lib.utoronto.ca/diana

National Offices

Amnesty International USA Women's Human Right Program
http://www.amnestyusa.org/women
Amnesty International USA
322 Eighth Avenue New York, NY 10001
Tel: (212) 807-8400; Fax: (212) 627-1451
E-mail: aimember@aiusa.orgemail

Center for Women's Global Leadership
http://www.cwgl.rutgers.edu
Center for Women's Global Leadership
Douglass College
Rutgers, The State University of New Jersey
160 Ryders Lane
New Brunswick, NJ 08901-8555 USA
Tel: (732) 932-8782; Fax: (732) 932-1180
Email: cwlg@igc.org

Freedom from Hunger
http://www.freefromhunger.org
Freedom from Hunger 1644 DaVinci Court Davis, CA 95616
Tel: (800) 708-2555; Fax: (530) 758-6241
E-mail: info@freefromhunger.org

Global Center for Women's Studies and Politics
http://glowboell.de/home/content/d/sitemap/index_html
Heinrich Böll Foundation
Rosenthaler Str. 40/4
10178 Berlin
Fon: (+30) 28534-0; Fax: (+30) 28534-109
E-mail: info@boell.de

Global Fund for Women
http://www.globalfundforwomen.org
The Global Fund for Women
1375 Sutter Street, Suite 400
San Francisco, California 94109 USA
Tel: (415) 202-7640 Fax: (415) 202-8604
E-mail: gfw@globalfundforwomen.org

Global Reproductive Health Forum – Harvard University
http :www.hsph.Harvard.edu/grhf/ Harvard School of Public Health
Department of Population and International Health
665 Huntington Avenue
Boston, MA 02115
Tel: (617) 432-4619
E-mail: jzucker@hsph.harvard.edu

The Heifer Project: Women in Development
http://www.heifer.org
Heifer Project International
P.O. Box 8058
Little Rock, AR/ USA 72203
Tel: (800) 422-0474
E-mail: info@heifer.org

International Women's Health Coalition
http://www.iwhc.org
International Women's Health Coalition
24 East 21st Street
New York, NY 10010, USA
Tel: (212) 979-8500; Fax: (212) 979-9009
E-mail: info@iwhc.org

NOW Foundation
http://nowfoundation.org
NOW Foundation
733 15th Street, NW
Washington, DC 20005
Tel: (202) 628-8669
Email: foundation@nowfoundation.org

Soroptimists International of the Americas
http://soroptimists.org
Soroptimists International of the Americas
Two Penn Plaza, Ste. 1000
Philadelphia, PA 19102 Tel: (215) 557-5300 Fax: (215) 568-5200
E-mail: siahq@soroptimist.org

Village Banking: Credit for Change
http://wwwvillagebanking.org
Village Banking Headquarters
1101 14th street, N.W., 11th Floor
Washington, D.C., 20005
Tel: (202) 682-1510; Fax: (202) 682-1535
E-mail: hnca@villagebanking.org

Women and International Development Program, Michigan State University
http://www.isp.msu.edu/wid/
Michigan State University
202 Center for International Programs
East Lansing, MI 48824-1 035
Tel: (517) 353-5040; Fax: (517) 432-4845
E-mail: WID@msu.edu

Women, Law and Development International
http://www.wld.org
WLDI
1350 Connecticut Ave., NW, Suite 1100
Washington, DC 20036
Tel: (202) 463-7477; Fax: (202) 463-7480
E-mail: wld@wld.org

Women's Environment and Development Organization (WEDO)
http://www.wedo.org
WEDO
355 Lexington Ave., 3rd Floor
New York, NY 10017
Tel: (212) 973-0325; Fax: (212) 973-0335
E-mail: wedo@wedo.org

A Website Devoted to Abolishing War

http://www.AFutureWithoutWar.org

The essays on this site:

- place a campaign to end war in historical context and assess how quickly it can achieve success
- explain why the empowerment of women is the key and the catalyst for any campaign to abolish war
- describe the nine interrelated goals that must be addressed simultaneously to achieve success

The site also provides more than 100 links to organizations already working on this effort.

Appendix II

Ways to Participate in Waging Peace

(*See also* the web site, A Future without War: www.afww.org)

These are basics. Some are easy, things we can all do if we simply think about them. Some require that you have leisure time. Many, not all, focus on empowering women. But all of them are things of which we should be mindful as we combine our energies and wills into a global effort to change our lives and future for the better.

> *There are thousands to tell you it cannot be done,*
> *There are thousands to prophesy failure;*
> *There are thousands to point out to you, one by one,*
> *The dangers that wait to assail you.*
> *But just buckle in with a bit of a grin,*
> *Just take off your coat and go to it;*
> *Just start to sing as you tackle the thing*
> *That "cannot be done," and you'll do it.*
>   ❧ Edgar A. Guest

Encourage young women in your life to achieve high goals. Let them know how important you consider them to be to humanity's future.

Encourage young men in your life to treasure their girlfriends, wives, and daughters and to be the first to encourage the women of their hearts to achieve.

Encourage your local, state, or even federal government to develop "initiation" programs for young people so that they know they belong, they are important, we are counting on them, and they have a vital stake in the future.

If the young people in your community cannot find work, ally yourself with others in your community who know this is dangerous and, working together, put wheels in motion to change that dire condition. And plan to stick with the effort over the long haul.

Be mindful of your own responsibility to educate yourself and vote—and do it.

If you have managed to make it "to the top" in any field, make a promise to yourself to look for competent women to mentor—and keep your promise.

Encourage educators and others dealing with young people to make clear to them, especially to young women, how important they are to the future and that their votes and behavior will be profoundly important.

Become familiar with the amount of your money, including your tax money, spent on:

- Waging War (this includes all forms of "defense" spending) versus
- Waging Peace (this includes funding for foreign aid) versus
- Seeking Pleasure (all the things we love to do but which do nothing to bring lasting stability – cosmetics, dining, sports, gambling, clothing, travel and on and on).

Women, Power, and the Biology of Peace

When you vote, of course vote for the best candidate, male or female. But if none of the names on the ballot are familiar or you don't know the candidates' positions, see if there is a woman, and vote for her.

And insist, through your voice in your community and your vote, that your leaders begin to put as much money, energy, and creativity into Waging Peace as they do into the many forms of Waging War. If they fail, then vote for someone who will.

Check your charitable giving to see how much is going to encourage empowerment of women in other countries, particularly developing countries. And make 50% of whatever you can give go to women and children elsewhere, in places where to empower them can make a major difference to our future.

Encourage older women and men—our "wise ones"—to enjoy their travel, golf, bridge, and tennis, but to also volunteer a portion of their time to whatever local causes help women, girls, or troubled young men. And make sure your community formally recognizes the importance of the efforts of our wise ones in this service.

If you are one of our wise ones, especially a woman, run for office—the school board, city council, maybe one of the county commissions. Maybe think big and long-term—head for even higher office. Add a female voice, your voice, to civic affairs.

Encourage young women to go into politics.

Encourage and embrace those changes in laws and customs that empower women—legally, educationally, and religiously. Never accept less. Never settle for less.

> *I am only one; but still I am one. I cannot do everything, but still I can do something. I will not refuse to do something I can do.*
> ❧ Helen Keller

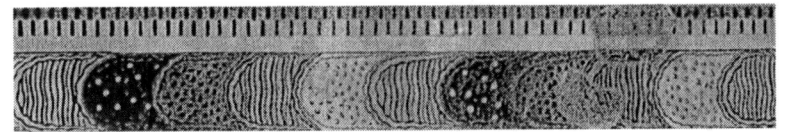

Selected References and Additional Recommended Reading

Introduction
As an example of the debate over **goddess societies**, see Goodison, Lucy & Christine Morris (eds.). *Ancient Goddesses: The Myths and the Evidence.*

Section I – Biology
A thorough discussion of and examples of **male and female reproductive strategies** can be found in Mealey, Linda. *Sex Differences: Developmental and Evolutionary Strategies.* E. O. Wilson's *Sociobiology* does not address this subject as directly, but it does provide a rich variety of descriptions of the behavior and adaptations of animals that illustrate how males and females of a wide variety of life forms behave so as to maximize their reproductive efforts over their lifetimes. Wilson is a fine starting place to explore basic theories of social evolution.

For the subject of **genes and evolution** see Richard Dawkins's *The Blind Watchmaker* for a clear description of how evolution works to produce anatomy and behavior. Ursula Goodenough, in *The Sacred Depths of Nature,* presents a succinct introductory view of how genes direct the construction of body parts like the brain or endocrine or sense organs.

Differences in brain structure citations are as follows:

- Pre-frontal cortex, web-thinking vs. step-thinking: Fisher, Helen. *The First Sex,* p. 9.
- Posterior temporal cortex: Blum, Deborah. *Sex on the Brain,* p. 60.
- Anterior commissure: Fisher, Helen. *The First Sex,* p. 11, and Blum, Deborah, *Sex on the Brain,* pp. 46-48.
- Corpus collosum: Fisher, Helen. *The First Sex,* p. 11, and Blum, Deborah, *Sex on the Brain,* pp. 46-48.
- INAH-3: Gilbert Susan. *A Field Guide to Boys and Girls,* p. 8; see also Blum, Deborah, *Sex on the Brain,* pp. 43-46.
- Rate of brain hemisphere development: Gilbert, Susan. *A Field Guide to Boys and Girls,* pp. 8, 24.

Differences in brain function citations are as follows:

- Laterality of function in men vs. women: Blum, Deborah. *Sex on the Brain,* pp. 46-47.
- Importance of effects of learning on the brain: Blum, Deborah, *Sex on the Brain,* Chapter 2.
- Differences in eye contact within hours of delivery: Gilbert, Susan. *A Field Guide to Boys and Girls,* p. 14.
- Frequency of crying: ibid, pp. 17-19.
- Fine motor skill development: ibid, p. 23.
- Language development: ibid, pp. 23-24.
- Emotional impulse control: ibid, pp. 27-29.
- Physical and verbal aggression: ibid, p. 38.
- Establishing dominance: ibid, pp. 58-60, and Fisher, Helen. *The First Sex,* Chapter 2.

The description of a **play session** comes from Tannen, Debra. *The Argument Culture*, p. 169.

Differential treatment of boys and girls is described in Gilbert, Susan. *A Field Guide to Boys and Girls*, pp. 16, 24-25, 44.

Section II – A Powerful, Creative Civilization without War – Is That Possible?

For descriptions of how **earthquakes and the explosion of Santorini** might have affected the Keftians see Pellegrino, Charles. *Unearthing Atlantis*, and Driessen, Jan and Colin MacDonald. *The Troubled Island*.

The quotation regarding the **Iroquois** comes from Ember, Carol and Melvin Ember. *Cultural Anthropology*, p. 152.

Aspects of **win-win or mutual gains bargaining** are discussed in, for example, Jandt, Fred E. *Win-win Negotiating: Turning Conflict Into Agreement*, and Ury, William. *Getting to Peace: Transforming Conflict at Home, at Work, and in the World*, (pp. 104-105).

Debra Tannen's description of the research of Sheldon on **how boys and girls resolve conflicts** is found in *The Argument Culture*, p. 174.

Detailed exploration of **kinship systems** can be found in Fox, Robin. *Kinship and Marriage: An Anthropological Perspective*. See also Ember and Ember's *Cultural Anthropology*.

Linear B tablets and what they can tell us about the time and place of the Keftians (Minoans) is explored in Chadwick, John. *The Mycenaean World*.

Section III – Regulating Social Behavior

Christopher Boehm's description of the use of **ostracism** by the Utku of Alaska and others is found in *Hierarchy in the Forest*, Chapter 3.

An introduction to **bonobos** is given in *Bonobo, The Forgotten Ape* by Franz de Waal and *The Last Ape*, by Takayoshi Kano. Jane

Women, Power, and the Biology of Peace

Goodall's *Through a Window: My Thirty Years with the Chimpanzees of Gombe* provides an introduction to **chimpanzees**.

Supernormal stimulus is defined and illustrated in Hinde, Robert, *Animal Behavior* (p. 68) in a section discussing animals' selective responsiveness to stimulation, pp. 58-7 1.

One of many books that describe the **benefits found in long-term, good marriages** is Wallerstein, Judith and Sandra Blakeslee. *The Good Marriage: How and Why Love Lasts.*

Section IV – Women And Warfare

For description of **how resources influence the relationships between the sexes** see Ember and Ember, *Cultural Anthropology*, pp. 154-156.

See Shostak, Marjorie. *Nisa. The Life and Words of a !Kung Woman* for description of female status (pp. 237-238) and the economic contribution (p. 240) of !Kung women.

For one view of **death rates and warfare in tribal cultures** see Keeley, Lawrence. 1996. *War Before Civilization.*

Yanomamö are described in Chagnon, Napoleon. *Yanomamö: The Fierce People.* The debate over Chagnon's work is discussed in Michael Shermer's article "Spin-doctoring the Yanomamö." See also Tierney, Patrick. *Darkness in El Dorado.*

Section V – Finding Solutions

The **egalitarian behavior of mated gulls** is described in Hand, J. L. 1985. "Egalitarian resolution of social conflicts: a study of pair-bonded gulls in nest duty and feeding contexts." Z. Tierpsychol. 70: 123-147. Also see Hand, J. L. 1986. "Resolution of Social Conflicts: Dominance, Egalitarianism, Spheres of Dominance and Game Theory," Quart. Rev. Biol. 61:201-220.

John Leo quote comes from CNN, 17 September 2001.

Joseph Biden quote comes from CNN's Hunt, Novak, and Shields, 13 October, 2001.

Sandra Bloom quote comes from L.A. Times, Oct. 7, 2001.
Fareed Zakaria quote from "Why do they hate us?" *Newsweek*, Oct. 15, 2001.
Joseph Campbell quote taken from Cohen, D. (Ed.). *The Circle of Life: Rituals From the Human Family.*
Oprah Winfry quote comes from L.A. Times, December 7, 2002.
Tony Blair quote comes from L.A. Times, February 24, 2003.
A good description of the **importance of connectedness to health and longevity** is Ornish, Dean. *Love and Survival: The Scientific Basis for the Healing Power of Intimacy.*

One example of books that look at the **disruptive influence of young males** is Schlegel, Alice, and Herbert Barry III. *Adolescence: An Anthropological Inquiry.*

For a casual look at the **Mosuo**, a web site of Göettner-Abendroth offers an introduction: http://promatriarchy.net/mosuo.html.

For their description of the **relationship between internal and external warfare and residence pattern**, see Ember and Ember, *Cultural Anthropology,* p. 191.

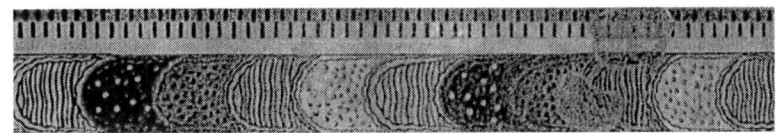

BIBLIOGRAPHY

Altmann, Jeanne. 1980. *Baboon Mothers and Infants.* Cambridge, Mass.: Howard University Press.
Blum, Deborah. 1997. *Sex on the Brain. The Biological Differences between Men And Women.* NY: Viking Penguin.
Boehm, Christopher. 1999. *Hierarchy in the Forest: The Evolution of Egalitarian Behavior.* Cambridge, Mass.: Harvard Univ. Press.
Chadwick, John. 1976. *The Mycenaean World.* New York: Cambridge University Press.
Chagnon, Napoleon A. 1977 *Yanomamö: The Fierce People.* NY: Holt, Rinehart and Winston.
Cohen, D. (Ed.). 1991. *The Circle of Life—Rituals from the Human Family.* London: The Aquarian Press.
Crocker, William H., and Jean Crocker. 1994. *The Canela: Bonding through Kinship, Ritual, and Sex.* Fort Worth: Harcourt Brace College Publishers.
Daly, Martin, and Margo Wilson. 1988. *Homicide.* Hawthorne, NY: Aldine de Gruyter.
Davis-Kimball, Jeannine. 1997. "Warrior women of the Eurasian steppes." Archaeology 50: 44-48.
Davis-Kimball, Jeannine and Mona Behan. 2002. *Warrior Women: An Archaeologist's Search for History's Hidden Heroines.* NY: Warner Books

Dawkins, Richard. 1986. *The Blind Watchmaker.* NY: Norton.
Diamond, Jared. 1992. *The Third Chimpanzee: The Evolution and Future of the Human Animal.* NY: HarperCollins.
Diamond, Jared. 1999, 1997. *Guns, Germs, and Steel: The Fates of Human Societies.* NY: W. W. Norton.
Driessen, Jan and Colin F. MacDonald. 1997. *The Troubled Island: Minoan Crete before and after the Santorini Eruption.* Aegaeum 17, Liige/Austin.
Ember, Carol R. and Melvin Ember. 1993. *Cultural Anthropology.* 7thEd. Englewood Cliffs, New Jersey: Prentice-Hall, Inc.
Eisler, Riane. 1987. *The Chalice and the Blade.* Cambridge, Mass.: Harper and Row.
────── 2007. *The Real Wealth of Nations: Creating a Caring Economics.* San Francisco: Berrett-Koehler Publishers, Inc.
Evans, Sir Arthur. 1921-35. *The Palace of Minos: An Account of the early Cretan Civilization as Illustrated by the Discoveries at Knossos.* London: Macmillan.
Fisher, Helen. 1992. *Anatomy of Love: The Natural History of Monogamy, Adultery, and Divorce.* NY: W. W. Norton & Company, Inc.
────── 1999. *The First Sex: The Natural Talents of Women and How They Are Changing the World.* NY: Random House. Fox,
Robin. 1967. *Kinship and Marriage: An Anthropological Perspective.* NY: Penguin.
Fry, Douglas P. 2006. *The Human Potential for Peace: An Anthropological Challenge to Assumptions about War and Violence.* NY: Oxford University Press.
────── 2007. *Beyond War: The Human Potential for Peace.* NY: Oxford University Press
Fukuyama, Francis. 1992. *The End of History and the Last Man.* New York: Free Press.
Gilbert, Susan. 2000. *A Field Guide to Boys and Girls.* NY: HarperCollins.

Goodall, Jane. 1990. *Through a Window: My Thirty Years with the Chimpanzees of Gombe.* Boston: Houghton Mifflin.

Goodenough, Ursula. 1998. *The Sacred Depths of Nature.* NY: Oxford University Press.

Goodison, Lucy & Christine Morris (eds.). 1998. *Ancient Goddesses: The Myths and the Evidence.* U. Of Wisconsin Press, Madison.

Gowatty Patricia Adair. 1997. *Feminism and Evolutionary Biology: Boundaries, Intersections, and Frontiers.* New York: Chapman & Hall : International Thomson Publication.

Gray, John. 1992. *Men Are from Mars, Women Are from Venus: A Practical Guide for Improving Communication and Getting What You Want in your Relationships.* New York: HarperCollins.

Hand, J. L. 1985. "Egalitarian resolution of social conflicts: a study of pair-bonded gulls in nest duty and feeding contexts." Z. Tierpsychol. 70: 123-147.

——— 1986. "Resolution of social conflicts: Dominance, egalitarianism, spheres of dominance and game theory." Quart. Rev. Biol. 61:201-220.

——— 2001. *Voice of the Goddess.* Cardiff, CA: Pacific Rim Press.

Hart, Michael H. 1978. *The 100: A Ranking of the Most Influential Persons in History.* NY: A & W Publishers, Inc.

Haviland, William A. 1999. *Cultural Anthropology.* 9th Ed. Orlando, Florida: Harcourt Brace & Company.

Hedges, Chris. 2002. *War is a Force That Gives Us Meaning.* NY: Public Affairs.

Hinde, Robert. 1970. *Animal Behaviour: A Synthesis of Ethology and Comparative Psychology.* McGraw-Hill.

Hoffman, Martin. 1978. "Sex differences in empathy and related behaviors." Psychology Bulletin 84: 7 12-722.

Hrdy, Sara Blaffer. 1999. *Mother Nature: a History of Mothers, Infants, and Natural Selection.* New York: Pantheon Books.

Hrdy, Sara Blaffer and Glenn Hausfater (eds.). 1984. *Infanticide: Comparative and Evolutionary Perspectives.* Hawthorne, NY: Aldine de Gruyter.

Hua, Cai. 2001. *A Society without Fathers or Husbands: the Na of China.* Translated by Asti Hustvedt. NY: Zone Books.

Jandt, Fred E. 1985. *Win-win Negotiating: Turning Conflict into Agreement.* NY: Wiley.

Kano, Takayoshi. 1992. *The Last Ape: Pygmy Chimpanzee Behavior and Ecology.* Translated by Evelyn Ono Vineberg. Stanford, CA: Stanford University Press.

Keeley, Lawrence. 1996. *War before Civilization: the Myth of the Peaceful Savage.* NY: Oxford Univ. Press.

Lancaster, Chet S. 1981. *The Goba of the Zambezi: Sex Roles, Economics and Change.* Norman: University of Oklahoma Press.

Lorenz, Konrad. 1974, c1966. *On Aggression.* Translated by Marjorie Kerr Wilson. New York: Harcourt Brace Jovanovich.

Mealey, Linda. 2000. *Sex Differences: Developmental and Evolutionary Strategies.* San Diego: Academic Press.

Moir, Anne and David Jessel. 1991. *Brain Sex. The Real Difference between Men and Women.* NY: Carol Publishing Group.

Muir, Kate. 1992. *Arms and the Woman. Female Soldiers at War.* London: Sinclair-Stevenson Ltd.

Nyborg, H. 1994. *Hormones, Sex and Society.* Westport, Conn.: Praeger.

Ornish, Dean. 1998. *Love and Survival. The Scientific Basis for the Healing Power of Intimacy.* NY: HarperCollins Publishers, Inc.

Pellegrino, Charles. 1991. *Unearthing Atlantis.* NY: Random House.

Salmonson, Jessica Amanda. 1991. *The Encyclopedia of Amazons: Women Warriors from Antiquity to the Modern Era.* NY: Paragon House.

Sanday, Peggy Reeves. 1981. *Women's Power and Male Dominance: on the Origins of Sexual Inequality.* NY: Cambridge University Press.

———— Forthcoming 2002. *Women at the Center: Life in a Modern Matriarchy.* Ithaca, NY: Cornell University Press.

Schiebinger, Londa. 1999. *Has Feminism Changed Science?* Cambridge, Mass: Harvard University Press.

Schlegel, Alice, and Herbert Barry III. 1991. *Adolescence: An Anthropological Inquiry.* NY: Free Press.

Shaywitz, B. A., S. E. Shaywitz, et. al. 1995. "Sex differences in the functional organization of the brain for language." Nature 373: 607-608.

Shermer, Michael. 2001. "Spin-doctoring the Yanomamö." In *Skeptic* 9: 36-47.

Shostak, Marjorie. 1983. Nisa. *The life and Words of a !Kung Woman.* NY: Random House.

Smuts, Barbara. 1985. *Sex and Friendship in Baboons.* Hawthorne, NY: Aldine.

Tannen, Debra. 1998. *The Argument Culture: Stopping America's War of Words.* NY: Ballantine.

Tierney, Patrick. 2000. *Darkness in El Dorado.* NY: Norton.

Ury, William. 1999. *Getting to Peace: Transforming Conflict at Home, at Work, and in the World.* NY: Viking.

Waal, Frans B. M. de. 1997. *Bonobo: the Forgotten Ape.* Berkeley: University of California Press.

Wallerstein, Judith S. and Sandra Blakeslee. 1995. *The Good Marriage: How and Why Love Lasts.* NY: Houghton Mifflin Co.

Waters, Frank. 1963. *Book of the Hopi.* New York: Penguin.

Wilson, E. O. 1975. *Sociobiology.* Cambridge: Harvard University Press.

Wrangham, Richard and Dale Peterson. 1996. *Demonic Males: Apes and the Origins of Human Violence.* NY: Houghton Mifflin.

Zakaria, Fareed. 2001. "Why do they hate us?" *Newsweek.* October 15.

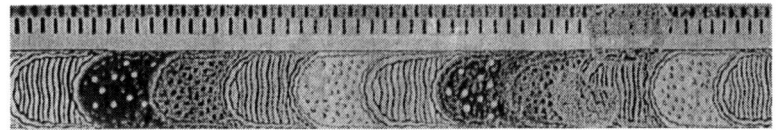

Index

About.com: Women's Issues: Third World, 155
Adolescence: An Anthropological Inquiry, (Schlegel and Barry), 167
A FutureWithoutWar (afww.org), x, 159
Afghanistan, 120, 122, 137
aggression,
 and neighbors, 71, 105, 149
 and sex, 79
 baboons, 115, 116
 bonobo, 80, 81
 chimpanzee, 80, 82, 83, 84
 controlling, 45, 99, 105, 118, 132, 133, 153, 164, 172
 cultural differences, 132
 domination, 109
 evolution of in humans, 28, 29, 81, 82, 116
 male/female differences, xiii, 25, 29, 41, 44–45, 131, 153
 Minoans (Keftians), 20, 68, 72, 77
 positive aspects, 151–52
 resources, 94
 verbal, 41
 war, 108, 118, 136
 warrior cultures, 132, 135
 young men, 131–132
agricultural revolution, 84, 93, 145
Agrippina the Elder, 100, 104
Akrotiri Town, 62, 86
Alexander the Great, 103, 152
alpha males, 114, 116

Altmann, Jeanne, 114, 115, 116
Altmann, Stewart, 114
Amazons, 96, 97
ambition. *See* recognition, need for
Amnesty International USA Women's Human Rights Program, 155
Anatomy of Love: The Natural History of Monogamy, Adultery, and Divorce. (Fisher), 145
Ancient Goddesses: The Myths and the Evidence (Goodison and Morris), 163
animal behavior, 114, 118, 151
Animal Behavior (Hinde), 166
anterior commissure, 37
Aphrodite, 87
Argentina, 99
Argument Culture, The: Stopping America's War of Words (Tannen), 41, 135, 165
Aristotle, 129, 130, 147
Arms and the Woman (Muir), 91, 95
art, keftian, 59–66, 69, 77, 85–86
Athens, 124
Atta, Mohamad, 129
Australia, 144
Aztec temples, 51

babies, 35, 36
Baboon Mothers and Infants (Altmann) 114
baboons, 26, 114, 115, 116, 117, 124
Bach, 102

175

balance, 21, 53, 62, 95, 143, 152, 153
ballot, 111
Barry, Herbert III, 167
battle. *See* war
Beethoven, 102
begging, by female gulls, 117, 118
behavior,
  and culture, 33,35, 43,58, 107, 121
  and evolution, 139, 147
  and the brain, 30
  animal, 151
  baboon, 115
  bonobo, 81
  chimpanzee, 81, 84
  egalitarian, 54, 84, 118
  human male, 44
  male/female differences, 35, 38, 41
  primate, 26
  regulating social behavior, 43, 54, 75, 77, 78, 79, 77–79
  sex differences, 36, 38, 40, 45, 55, 118
  sexual, 81
bell curve, 31, 32, 38, 104
Bernieres, Louis de, 23
Bernstein, Irwin, 114
bias
  author, xiv
  investigator, 36, 63, 69
Biden, Joseph, 120, 137, 166
Bill and Melinda Gates Foundation, 133
biological logic, 26
biological logic behind male/female inclinations, the, 26–29
biological priorities, 29, 118, 147
biology, xiv, xv, 21, 25, 57, 59, 128, 139, 147
  evolutionary, xiv, 25
Blair, Tony, 150, 167
Blakeslee, Sandra, 166
blame for war, 147
Blind Watchmaker, The (Dawkins), 163
Bloom, Sandra, 126, 167
Bluebird, The, 66

Blum, Deborah, 26, 37, 39, 40, 42, 164
Boehm, Christopher, 43, 54, 55, 78, 82, 83, 94, 118, 165
Bolivar, Simon, 103
Bonaparte, Napoleon, 103, 152
bonding, 31, 45, 81, 83, 84, 85, 126, 152, 153
Bonobo, The Forgotten Ape (Wall de), 165
bonobos, 58, 79, 80, 81, 82, 83, 88, 165
  biological traits shared with humans, 82, 83
boys, 36, 38, 40, 41, 42, 55, 131, 132
brain, 26, 36, 37, 38, 39, 40
  function, 29–30, 32, 38–39, 40, 41, 164
  sex differences, 35, 36, 37, 38
  structure, 29, 30, 32, 35–38, 40, 41, 164
Brain Sex (Moir and Jessel), 37
breasts, 31, 60, 63, 64, 85, 86
Bronze Age, 19, 20, 51, 64, 86
Brown, Antoinette, 141
Buddha, 102
Bull Leapers, The, 60
bull, bull-leaping, 20, 53, 60, 63, 68

Caesar, Augustus, 103, 152
Campbell, Joseph, 167
Canela, 84, 89
Canela, The: Social Bonding through Ritual, Kinship, and Sex (Crocker and Crocker), 84
capitalism, 43
carrot, 75, 77, 79
Catherine the Great, 104
cells, 29, 39, 40, 41
Center for Women's Global Leadership, 156
Chadwick, John, 165
Chagnon, Napoleon, 106, 166
Chalice and The Blade, The (Eisler), 18
charitable giving, 161

Women, Power, and the Biology of Peace

Chase, Stuart, 75
child-bearing, 73, 94
  and women's breasts, 85
childcare, 144
children,
  and bussing, 43–44
  and resources, 57, 59, 89
  a peaceful future for, 108
  costs to raise, 27
  cross-cultural studies of, 32, 39–40
  determining parentage of, 57
  differential treatment of, 36
  flower children, 77, 81
  foot-binding, 139
  legal access to after divorce, 140, 143
  of God, 141
  parents being connected to, 126, 127, 129
  sexual differences, 40–42
  sexual differences in play session, 41
chimpanzees, 26, 57, 58, 79, 80, 81, 82, 83, 84, 88, 106, 114, 166
China, 149
chivalrous nature, 97, 100, 102
Churchill, Odette, 96
Churchill, Winston, 17, 109, 111
Circle of Life, The: Rituals From the Human Family (Cohen), 167
Cleopatra, 104, 123
Clinton, Bill, xiii, 120
clitoris, 82
communism, 43, 121, 128
community-based societies, 50, 53, 71, 72, 121
computer games, 132
conflict, 4, 55, 56, 70, 72, 73, 80, 89, 97, 102, 108, 119, 135, 136, 138, 141, 152
conflict resolution, 135
  benefits of reconciliation, 152
  debate vs. dialogue mentality, 135
  lose-lose, 55, 106, 108
  mutual gains bargaining, 55, 165

  non-violent, 134
  other cultures, 135
  third side mediators, 135
  win-lose, 56, 134, 135
  win-win, 55, 56, 108, 120, 134, 136, 137, 165
Confucius, 102
Congregationalist Church, 141
connectedness
  need for, 88, 125–129, 131, 133, 134, 138, 167
  need for (negatively met), 127
  need for connectedness (positively met) as an engine of history, 124, 125–27
conquerors, 102, 103, 104
conquest, 69, 71, 93, 100, 104, 128, 136
continuous receptivity, 58, 82
Copernicus, 102
Corelli's Mandolin (Bernieres), 23
Corinth, 87
corpus collosum, 37
Coulson, John, 117
Crete, 18, 19, 20, 21, 51, 65, 66, 67, 68, 69, 71, 72, 88, 105, 170
crimes, young males, 131
Crocker, William and Jean, 84
Cromwell, Oliver, 103
cross-cultural studies, 32, 39, 40, 131, 149
Cultural Anthropology (Ember and Ember), 32, 165, 166
culture/s, 19, 27, 93, 99, 139
  American, 25, 132
  and art, 65
  and goddesses, 18, 61
  and young males, 132–133
  as determinants of behavior, 33, 35, 40, 42, 43, 78
  community-based, 50, 53
  complexity and war, 105
  cultural differences, 28, 32, 88, 132, 135

egalitarian, 54, 118
male dominated/patriarchal, xiv, 19, 54, 57, 80
matrilineal, 58
matrilocal, 58
Minoan/Keftian/Cretan, 20, 51, 52, 66, 68, 69–73, 79
tribal/hunter-gatherer, 53, 54, 106
woman-centered, 53, 79, 148–150

Dahomey, Kingdom of, 97
Daly, Martin, 131
Darkness in El Dorado (Tierney), 166
Darwin, 102
Davis-Kimball, Jeannine, 96, 97
Dawkins, Richard, 163
death rates, 105, 106, 166
decision-making affecting the community or state, xiv, 50, 52, 53, 54, 71, 120, 128, 148, 150
defense, 31, 42, 68, 99, 100, 101, 103, 105, 106, 107
defense vs. offense and women, 45, 97, 98, 99–104
democracy,
 and women, 50, 128, 137, 138, 139, 142, 143, 144
 control of resources, 72
 election of Hitler, 142
 failure of ancient/classical, 124, 128
 Fukuyama, 121–123, 127
 means to restrain (male) urge to dominate, 43, 133, 139, 142, 153
 pivotal to fostering peace, 108–109
Demonic Males: Apes and the Origins of Human Violence (Wrangham and Peterson), 81
Devore, Irven, 114
Diamond, Jared, 80, 93
divorce, 59, 140, 143, 146
DNA, 80
dominance, 41, 43, 55, 80, 114, 115, 117, 118, 124

dominance hierarchy, 43, 55, 80, 81, 115, 116, 124
dominance, male, 21, 80, 81, 82, 84, 114
drains, Keftian, 19, 65
Driessen, Jan, 69, 165

earthquakes, Keftian, 69, 165
Edison, Thomas, 102
education, 17, 44, 137, 138, 140, 142, 143
egalitarian, 19, 43, 54, 55, 83, 84, 105, 107, 137, 149, 166
Einstein, Albert, 102
Eisler, Riane, 18, 19, 139
Elizabeth I, 72, 102, 104
Ember, Carol and Melvin, 33, 54, 149, 165, 166
empowerment of women
 economic, 139
 educational, 138
 legal, 140
 religious, 140
 worldwide, 141
Encyclopedia of Amazons, The (Salmonson), 96, 97
End of History and the Last Man, The (Fukuyama), 47, 121
end-of-life care, 145
environmentalists, 136
epiphany, 35, 36
equal pay for equal work, 144
ethos, 71, 134, 135
 non-violent, 71, 77
Europe, 18, 64, 65, 144, 145
Evans, Sir Arthur, 19, 20, 49, 60, 63, 64, 69
evolution,
 brains/inclinations, 30
 chimpanzee and bonobo differences, 81
 egalitarian behavior, 54
 female urge for social stability, 29, 45
 hidden ovulation, 58

human social origins, 82–84, 147
male aggression, 28–29, 116
male bonding and aggression, 45
resources, importance of, 28, 57
sex differences in behavior, 38
women's collaboration in patriarchy, 139
evolutionary biology, 26
exposing newborn girls, 139
eye color measurement, 31

facial expressions in Keftian art, 66
Falklands, 99
fascism, 121, 128
female empowerment
  bonobo and human physical similarities, 81–84
Feminism and Evolutionary Biology: Boundaries, Intersections, and Frontiers (Gowaty, ed.), 119
feminists, 47
fertility, 28, 57, 58, 73, 82, 83
fertilization, 83
Field Guide to Boys and Girls, A (Gilbert), 40, 164, 165
Finnland, 144
First International Minoan Celebration of Partnership, The, 18
First Sex, The (Fisher), 37, 55, 56, 107, 136, 164, 165
Fisher, Helen, 37, 38, 55, 56, 107, 136, 145, 146, 164
flush toilets, 65
focal animal sampling, 101, 114, 115
foot-binding, 138–139
fortification, 68
Fox, Robin, 165
Freedom From Hunger, 156
freedom of speech, 124
free love, 84
friendship, 152
Fry, Douglas, 50, 108, 132

Fukuyama, Francis, 47, 121, 122, 123, 124, 127, 129, 130
future, the nature of the, 142–46

geese, 118
gender, xiv, 31, 32, 35, 39, 40, 62
genetic, 26, 45, 81
Genghis Khan, 103, 152
Germans, 17, 91, 96, 98, 142
Getting to Peace: Transforming Conflict at Home, at Work, and in the World (Ury), 108, 135, 165
Gilbert, Susan, 40, 42, 164, 165
Girl from Akrotiri, 66
Girl with Shaved Head, 66
girls,
  behavioral and physical differences from boys, 38, 40–42, 55–56, 131, 132
  Canela girls and sex, 85
  Dahomy girls as warriors, 98
  different treatment of boys and, 36
  foot-binding, exposure,
  infundibulation, 139
  Oprah's academy, 137
Global Center for Women's Studies and Politics, 156
global community, 109
Global Fund for Women, 156
Global Reproductive Health Forum, 156
Goba, 53, 149
Goba of the Zambezi, The: Sex Roles, Economics and Change (Lancaster), 149
god, 61, 63
goddess, 53, 61, 62, 63, 64, 72, 86, 87, 99, 141
goddess societies, 18, 163
Gods Must Be Crazy, The (film), 94
Göettner-Abendroth, Heidi, 149, 167
Good Marriage, The: How and Why Love Lasts (Wallerstein and Blakeslee), 166

Goodall, Jane, 165–166
Goodenough, Ursula, 164
Goodman, Robert, x
Goodison, Lucy, 163
gorillas, 26, 80, 114
Göttner-Abendroth, Heidi, 148
Gournia, 64
Gowaty, Patricia, *119*
Gray, John, 25
Great Central Court, 20
Great Wall of China, 51
Greeks, 19, 49, 61, 64, 65, 68, 87, 88, 96, 97
guarding females, 82, 116
Guest, Edgar A., 159
gulls, 85, 86, 117, 118, 124, 166
guns, 132
Guns, Germs, and Steel (Diamond), 93

Habitat for Humanity, 133
Hand, Judith L., 166
Hanging Gardens of Babylon, 50
harem, for males, 151
harmony, 79, 89, 135, 153
Hart, Michael, 102, 103, 104
Harvester Vase, 66
Hatfields and McCoys, 106
Hausfater, Glen, 28
Haviland, William, 33
headdress, 63
Hedges, Chris, 45, 120
Heifer Project, The: Women in Development, 157
Heraklion, 18, 19
herding. *See* guarding females
heroines, 100
hidden females, 32, 114, 116, 119–120, 124
hidden ovulation, 57, 58, 82
Hierarchy in the Forest: A Study of Egalitarian Cultures Worldwide (Boehm), 43, 54, 118, 165
high priestess, 53, 62, 72

Hinde, Robert, 166
Hippocrates, 96
history,
  end of, 47, 121–122, 123–124, 125, 127, 136
  lack of peace in male dominated cultures, viii, 138, 153
  male warriors in, 102–103, 104
  patriarchies the subject of written history, 47, 79
  tide of history changing, xv
  women warriors in, 97, 99–102, 104
Hitler, Adolph, 103, 142
Hoffman, Martin, 42
Hollywood, films, 132
Homicide (Daly and Wilson), 131
Homo sapiens, 80, 143, 150
Hopi, 71, 132
Hormones, Sex and Society (Nyborg), 131
hospice. *See* end-of-life-care
Hrdy, Sara Blaffer, 26, 28, 55, 139
Hua, Cai, 27, 149
human nature, xiv, 43, 44, 52, 118, 146
  outer boundaries of behavior, 44, 43–44, 146
humanity, xiv, 17, 20, 51, 118, 124, 142
hunter-gatherers, 53, 54, 55, 84, 94, 105, 145
Hussein, Saddam, 95, 150
hydrogen atoms, 39

Iliad (Homer), 64
INAH-3, sexual desire, 40
inclinations, 105, 121, 153.
  and the bell curve, 31–32
  evolutionary origins, 26–29
  female, 29, 30, 42, 45, 72, 99, 128, 136, 150, 151, 153
  for peace, 71
  for war or social stability, 32

genetics of, 29–30
male, 29, 30, 45, 55, 153
male/female differences, 33
infanticide, 28, 80, 81
Infanticide (Hrdy and Hausfater), 28
infants, 32, 39, 40, 42
inferior frontal gyrus, 39
infundibulation, 58, 139
initiation, 133, 134
innate, 32, 44
Inquisition, the, 103
international community, doctrine of, 150
International Women's Health Coalition, 157
intuition, 38
invade and conquer, 25, 29
Iraq, 135, 150
Iroquois, 50, 54, 165
Isabella I, 102, 103
isotope, radioactive. *See* radioactive isotope

Jandt, Fred. E., 165
Jehovah's Witnesses, 78
Jessel, David, 37
Jesus, 102
Judaism, 141

Kano, Takayoshi, 81, 165
Keeley, Lawrence, 166
Keftian dress, 85, 86
Keftians,
  art and the status of women, 60–64
  art indicating cultural spirit, 65–66
  artifacts indicate sophisticated culture, 64–65
  earthquakes, 69, 165
  evidence suggesting no warfare, 66–70
  exceptional/lacking war unique, 50, 51, 67, 68, 69
  language, 51, 68
  love not war, 88

location/time/decline, 51
marines/navy, 67–68
matriarchy, 52–53
matrilineal, 56–58
matrilocal, 58–59
necessary conditions for peace, 70–73, 105
origins of the name Keftian, 49
regulating social behavior, 74, 79
religion, 52
snake goddesses/sacred sex hypothesis, 85–87
war not required for social/cultural sophistication, 67
Keller, Helen, 161
king, 19, 49, 63, 64, 69, 98
kingships, 121, 128
Kinship and Marriage: An Anthropological Perspective (Fox), 165
kinship systems, 165
Knossos, 19, 49, 51, 61, 63, 64, 65, 71, 72
  temple, 64
Kubler-Ross, Elizabeth, 145
!Kung San, 94, 132, 166

Lancaster, Chet, 53, 149
Lao Tzu, 102
Last Ape, The (Kano), 165
lateralized, 38
Laws, The (Plato), 130
learning, 32, 33, 40, 42, 148
legal protection, 144
Lenin, Nicoli, 103
Leo, John, 119, 166
Levy, Jerre, 36
Lincoln, Abraham, 111
Linear A, 51, 68
Linear B, 61, 165
linguistic abilities, 31, 37, 39, 41
Litvak, Lily, 91, 98
Lorenz, Konrad, 118, 123, 151, 152
love, 152

Love and Survival: The Scientific Basis for the Healing Power of Intimacy (Ornish), 167
MacDonald, Colin, 69, 165
Machiavelli, 103
Machu Picchu, 51
Mahavira, 102
male bonding, 108, 153
male-dominated government, failure to bring peace, xiii
male/female reproductive strategies, 26, 163
male-dominated culture, xiv
male-dominated industries, 142
Mao Tse-tung, 103
marriage, 27, 58, 59, 88, 89, 117, 144, 146, 149, 152, 166
Mars, 25, 93
math/spatial ability, 31, 39, 41
matriarchy,
  a peaceful alternative, 47
  family matriarch, 59
  no historical precedent, 47, 52–53, 148
Matriarchy (Göetter-Abendroth), 149
matrilineal, 56, 57, 58, 148
matrilocal, 52, 56, 58, 59, 148, 149, 150
  relation to female empowerment, 58–59
McNamara, Robert, ix
Mealey, Linda, 37, 163
megalothymos, 104, 123, 128, 152
Meir, Golda, 99
men,
  aggression, 45, 79, 94, 151
  and religion, 141
  and sex, 79, 84, 85, 87–89, 152
  and war, 103, 106, 137, 146, 152, 153
  and women and bell curves, 31–32, 104
  conflict resolution, 55
  dominance/power-seeking/recognition, 55, 123, 124
  effects of culture on, 42, 54
  egalitarian contexts, 54, 55, 94, 149
  famous/great, 102–103
  feelings about war versus love, 152
  governance by, xiii, 50, 53–54, 153
  how different from women, 32, 37–39, 41, 55–56, 103, 118, 119, 123, 124, 136
  how similar to women, 32, 95, 118, 124, 125, 136
  long-term planning, 56, 136
  Martian, 25
  our experts, 114, 129–131
  partnership with women, xiv, 19, 21, 149, 153
  social stability, 31
  unique individuals, 32
  young, difficulties with, 127, 131–32
  young, ways to help, 132–34
Men are from Mars, Women are from Venus (Gray), 25
Mennonites, 78
mentoring, 160
metals, 71
Michelangelo, 102
militant enthusiasm. *See* recognition, need for
Minangkabau, 148, 149
minds, of men and women, 36, 39
Minoan, 18, 19, 20, 21, 49, 50, 51, 66, 165
  no written history, 68
Minos, 19, 49, 63, 64
misconduct, human, 77
Mixed Audience, 62
Mohammad, 102
Moir, Anne, 37
money, 134, 160
moral, 17, 21, 54, 124, 134, 137, 147
Morris, Christine, 163
Mosuo, 27, 149, 167
Mother Nature (Hrdy), 26, 28, 55, 57, 139
Moynihan, Martin, 117

MRI, magnetic resonance imaging, 39, 40
Muir, Kate, 91, 95, 96, 97, 98
multitasking, 38
murder, 80, 81, 84
Mycenaean World, The (Chadwick), 165
Mycenaeans, 64
mythology, 52

nature, 66, 126, 129
nature vs. nurture, 35, 40
navy, 53, 67, 69, 105
necessary conditions, 70, 108, 134
needs, fundamental, 72, 124
negotiation, 71, 135
neurobiologist, 36
New Zealand, 144
Newton, Isaac, 102
Nietzsche, Friedrich, 123, 130
Nisa. The life and words of a !Kung woman (Shostak), 94, 166
nonviolent, 107
Northern Ireland, 106
NOW Foundation, 157
Nyborg, H., 131, 172

On Aggression (Lorenz), 118, 123, 151
Ornish, Dean, 167
Osama bin Ladin, 120
ostracism, 54, 77, 78, 165
ovulation, hidden, 57, 58, 82

pacifism, pacifists, 17, 18, 19
pain, acute, 38
palace of Minos, 19, 49, 63, 64
Palestine, 106
Papandreou, Margarita, 19
Papio cyanocephalus (yellow baboon), 114
partnership, male/female, xiv, 19, 21, 153
Paschal, Blaise, 130
paternity, 57, 58, 115, 145

patriarchal, 18, 19, 47, 52, 57, 58, 80, 105, 106, 107, 137, 141
patriarchy, 52, 53, 54, 58, 79, 88, 139, 148
patrilineal, 57
patrilocal, 59, 149, 150
peace, 109
  conditions for, 21, 108, 109
  Keftian, 20, 66, 68, 71, 72, 79
  Iroquois women, 54
  tendency to make/seek, 32, 44, 45, 47, 136
  waging peace, 108, 109, 129, 135, 143, 153, 159–161
  women-centered cultures, 149
  world, 21, 29, 108, 120, 136, 141, 142, 147
peaceableness, bonobos, 81, 83
Pellegrino, Charles, 69, 165
penchant. *See* inclinations
PET, positron emission tomography, 39, 40
Peterson, Dale, 81, 82, 83
Phaestos, 64
Picasso, Pablo, 102
planning ahead, 38, 56, 72, 107, 136, 138
Plato, 102, 123, 129, 130, 131, 147
politics, 161
population density, 72
posterior temporal cortex, 37
Potnia, 61
Powell, Colin, 137
power,
  and matrilineality, 58
  and matrilocality, 58–59
  at Knossos, 71
  dominance/thymos/spiritedness/power-seeking, 123
  Keftian women, 52, 60, 62
  male/female differences, 55–56, 122
  of religion, 72, 78

seductive sway of, 25
shared, 53, 54, 150
sources of, 59, 73, 93–94, 118–119
snake goddesses, symbolism, 86
women, 50, 54, 55, 56, 100, 104
power-seeking. *See* recognition, need for pre-frontal cortex, 37
primate, 26, 27, 28, 57, 78, 85, 99, 100, 114, 126
Prince, The, 63
priorities, men vs. women, 107
Procession, The, 20, 61, 63
Protestant, 141
protons, 39
punishment, 77, 78
Pylos, 64
pyramids, Egyptian, 50

Quakers, 132

radio frequency pulse. *See* MRI, magnetic resonance imaging
rank, 43, 100, 115, 116, 117, 151
rape, 106
Real Wealth of Nations, The, (Eisler), 139–140
receptivity, continuous, 57, 83
recognition, need for, 104, 123, 124, 125, 127, 128, 131, 132
need for as an engine of history, 123
reinforcers of behavior, 30, 45, 78, 79
religion, 17, 52, 71, 72, 78, 79, 86, 87, 119, 122, 126, 140, 141, 147
religious ecstasy, 66
reproduction, as an expensive process, 27
reproductive strategies, 26
reproductive success, 27, 45, 114
republic, 124, 127
resources, 17, 27, 28, 50, 53, 54, 57, 59, 64, 71, 72, 83, 88, 93, 94, 105–106, 107, 108, 118–119, 134, 143, 144, 147, 153, 155, 166

revenge, revenge cycles, 105, 106, 108
revolution, giving women the vote, 50
revolutionaries, 103, 104
reward, 77, 79
rhyming task. *See* linguistic abilities
ridicule, 54
risk-taking, 38
rites of passage, 132, 133
roads, Keftian paved roads, 65
romantic love, 88, 89
Roosevelt, Theodore, 75
rough and tumble play, 40
rules, 84, 85, 89, 115

Sacred Depths of Nature, The (Goodenough), 164
sacred sex hypothesis, 79, 84
evidence for, 79–81, 84–88
Salmonson, Jessica Amanda, 96, 97, 98, 99, 100, 102, 103, 104
Sanday, Peggy Reeves, 50, 148
Santorini, 51, 69, 165
Saunders, Dame Cicely, 145
Sauromatian women, 96
Schiebinger, Londa, 119
Schlegel, Alice, 167
scientific method, 119, 131, 146, 147
as an engine of history, 122
Search for Atlantis, The (Pellegrino), 69
secular morality, 17
secular system of laws, 78
Semiramis, 104
sense organs, 29
sequestration, of women, 58
sex,
and romantic love, 89
as social bonding mechanism, 83, 84
basic need for, 123, 125
bonobos, 80–81
changes in practices and attitudes, 144
frontal, bonobos and humans, 82
Keftian snake goddesses and, 86
rules to regulate, 85, 89

sacred, 79, 87, 88
Sex and Friendship in Baboons (Smuts), 116
Sex Differences: Developmental and Evolutionary Strategies (Mealey), 37, 163
Sex on the Brain (Blum), 26, 37, 40, 164
Shaywitz, Sally and Bennett, 39
Sheldon, Amy, 55
Shostak, Majorie, 94, 166
shunning, 54, 77, 78, 79
siege, 68, 100
Smith, Susan, 117
Smuts, Barbara, 116
snake goddesses, 79, 86
Snake Goddesses, 85
social engineering, 44
social stability,
  a female priority/inclination, 29, 127, 153
  and conflict resolution, 135, 138
  and genes, 29
  and young males, 84, 131, 133
  conditions necessary for, 70–73, 120, 123, 124, 138, 153
  Keftian, 66
  potential male/female differences, 32
  taken to excess by women, 151
societies, state-level, 52, 127, 135
Society Without Fathers and Husbands, A (Hua), 149
Sociobiology (Wilson), 163
Socrates, *124*
Spanish Armada, 105
Special Operations Executive (SOE), 95, 96
Stalin, 103
state-level civilization, 20, 49, 50, 51, 60, 64, 70, 71, 72, 106, 121
status. *See* dominance hierarchy
  humans, female, 55, 98, 100, 101
  humans, general, 43, 57, 59, 94, 123, 126, 127

humans, male, 55, 131
non-human primates, 80, 115, 116
stick, 75, 77, 78
subjugation, 68
subordination, 84, 124, 147
suffrage, 142
super-normal stimulus, 85, 86, 166
Swallows, The, 66
swingers, 89
Szabo, Violet, 96

tabula rasa, 35
take up arms, 99, 100, 101, 102, 103, 104
Tannen, Debra, 41, 55, 135, 165
temple, 4, 64, 87, 88
tendencies, 14, 31, 32, 38, 44, 80, 120, 136, 142. *See* inclinations
  female, 30, 72
  male, 28, 30, 44, 108
terraces, agricultural, 69
testosterone, 41, 131
Thatcher, Margaret, 99
The 100: A Ranking of the Most Influential Persons in History (Hart), 102
theocracy, 142
Thera. *See* Santorini
Third Chimpanzee, The (Diamond), 80
Through a Window: My Thirty Years with the Chimpanzees of Gombe (Goodall), 166
thymos, 123, 132. *See* recognition, need for
Tierney, Patrick, 166
Tinbergen, Nikko, 117
totalitarianism, *128*
tribal, 50, 52, 53, 54, 71, 72, 84, 105, 106, 120, 121, 135
Troubled Island, The (Driessen and MacDonald), 69, 165
Ts'ai Lun, 102

Umar ibn al-Khattab, 103

• *185* •

Women, Power, and the Biology of Peace

Unearthing Atlantis (Pellegrino), 165
United States, 27, 50, 120, 122, 132, 137, 141, 142, 144
upstart males, 54, 94, *119*
Ury, William, 108, 135, 165
Utku, 78, 165
utopia, 77
vagina, 82
Venus, 25, 93
video games, 132
Village Banking: Credit for Change, 158
Voice of the Goddess, 20
volcano, Santorini, 51
vote,
  by women, a revolutionary precedent, 50
  in liberal democracies, 123, 128
  tool that restrains domination/aggression, 109, 142
  tool for social change, 108, 137, 138, 139, 142, 153, 160, 161
  women, 50, 128, 137, 138, 139, 142, 144, 161

Waal, Franz de, 165
Wallerstein, Judith, 166
walls, retaining, 69
war,
  addictive quality of, 45, 120
  a future without, ia, ib, 159
  against terrorism, 108
  and genes, 29
  and men, 23, 50, 102–104, 121, 132, 152–153
  and women's reproductive priorities, 27
  and residence patterns, 150
  and resources, 73, 93, 105
  and sex, 79
  and women, 20, 95, 99, 54, 97, 98, 104, 105, 107
  and women-centered cultures, 150
  as a choice, xv, 30, 146, 147, 152
  beneficial, necessary evil, xiv, 49
  biological roots of, 28–29, 108, 147
  blame for, 146–147
  causes of, 70, 79, 108, 121, 123, 129, 131–132, 134, 147, 152
  chimpanzees, 80
  creative civilization without, 47, 49, 60, 67, 68–70, 105
  cure for, 121
  inevitability, ix-x, 18, 108
  Make love not war, 88
  male/female differences, 32, 33, 103–104, 118
  necessary, xiv, 18, 95
  of conquest/aggression vs. defense, 97, 99, 100, 101
  preemptive, 107
  prevention of, 108, 121, 132–134, 135, 136–138, 138–142, 147, 125–129, 150, 153
  proximal causes of, 151
  reasons women support a war, 105–107
  tribal, 105–106
  women as the desired resource, 106
War Before Civilization (Keeley), 166
War is a Force that Gives Us Meaning (Hedges), 45, 120
warfare,
  Afghan male-led, 137
  and the modern ethos, 135
  and type of residence pattern, 149
  internal vs. external, 149–150, 167
  Keftians, 51, 66 68, 69–70
  non-human primates, 81, 84
  Women in modern war, 95
warlords, 120
warrior cultures, 44, 64, 100, 132, 135
Warrior Women: An Archaeologist's Search for History's Hidden Heroines (Davis-Kimball), 97
warriors, 102, 104, 106, 107, 132
wars of
  aggression, conquest, 97, 99, 102, 105
  defense, 97

Washburn, Sherwood, 114
Washington, George, 103
watchtowers, 69
Waters, Frank, 71
weapons, 68, 69, 70, 73, 94
web-thinking vs. step-thinking, 37
West Sumatra, Indonesia, 148
Wicca, 141
Williams, Robin, 17
Wilson, E. O., 163
Wilson, Margo, 131
Winfry, Oprah, 137, 167
Win-win Negotiating: Turning Conflict Into Agreement (Jandt), 165
"wise ones", 161
women,
 Afghan, 120, 137–138
 and aggression, 132
 and changing customs, 145–146
 and conquest, 100–102, 103–104
 and defense, 99, 100
 and economics, 139–140, 143
 and education, 138–139, 143, 144
 and end-of-life care, 145
 and genetics, 45
 and law, 140, 144
 and men and bell curves, 31–32
 and military life, 95
 and motherhood, 25, 58
 and power, 20, 55, 59, 94, 122, 123
 and religion, 140–141
 and sex, 144
 as collaborators with men, 138–139, 146
 as scientists, 119
 biological priorities, 29, 118
 Canela, and sex, 84–85
 catalysts for social change, 70
 central figures, Keftian art, 20, 60, 61–62, 64
 collaboration with patriarchy, 139, 146
 Chorinthian, and sacred sex, 87
 conflict resolution, 55
 curbing male aggression/domination, 54, 128, 153
 empowering worldwide, 141–142, 155–158
 empowering women beyond politics, 138–142
 governance by, 49
 how different from men, 26, 37–39, 41, 45, 118, 120, 124, 130
 how like men, 36
 hidden ovulation/continuous receptivity, 57–58
 initiation of, 133–134
 internet resources to aid women, 155
 Keftian, 20, 49, 52, 60–62, 86, 88
 long-term planning, 56, 136
 power sharing/partnership with men, xiv, 21, 53–54, 136, 143, 147, 153
 recognition of need to empower women, 120, 136–38
 social stability, 29, 45, 72, 124, 128, 151, 153
 status, 55, 94
 unique individuals, 32
 Venusian, 25
 voting, 50, 128, 138, 142, 143, 144, 153
 warriors, 32, 42, 95, 96, 97, 98, 100
Women and International Development Program, 158
Women, Law, and Development International, 158
Women, Power, and the Biology of Peace (Hand), xi, xv, 20, 21, 33, 113
women-centered cultures, 53, 107, 148–150
Women's Environment and Development Organization (WEDO), 158
Women's Human Rights Net, 155
Women's Human Rights Resources, 155
Women's Liberation Movement, 33, 61
word tasks. *See* linguistic abilities

work, importance for social stability, 134, 160
World Trade Center, 119, 126, 129
Wrangham, Richard, 81, 82, 83
Xenobia, 100, 104
Yanomamö, 166
Yanomamö: The Fierce People (Chagnon), 106, 166

young male syndrome, the, 131
young males, 40, 84, 115, 131, 132, 133, 134, 147, 167
YouthBuild USA, 133

Zakaria, Fareed, 131, 167

Printed in the United States
127756LV00001B/2/P